Al
O
CAUTION: I
that this play is subject to royalty. It is fully protected by Original Works Publishing, and the copyright laws of the United States. All rights, including professional, amateur, motion pictures, recitation, lecturing, public reading, radio broadcasting, television, and the rights of translation into foreign languages are strictly reserved.

The performance rights to this play are controlled by Original Works Publishing and royalty arrangements and licenses must be secured well in advance of presentation. PLEASE NOTE that amateur royalty fees are set upon application in accordance with your producing circumstances. When applying for a royalty quotation and license please give us the number of performances intended, dates of production, your seating capacity and admission fee. Royalties are payable with negotiation from Original Works Publishing.

Royalty of the required amount must be paid whether the play is presented for charity or gain and whether or not admission is charged. Particular emphasis is laid on the question of amateur or professional readings, permission and terms for which must be secured from Original Works Publishing through direct contact.

Copying from this book in whole or in part is strictly forbidden by law, and the right of performance is not transferable.

Whenever the play is produced the following notice must appear on all programs, printing, and advertising for the play:

**"Produced by special arrangement with
Original Works Publishing.
www.originalworksonline.com"**

Due authorship credit must be given on all programs, printing and advertising for the play.

About the cover: From the Marquette University production. Photo by Kevin Pauly; Set Design by Stephen Hudson-Mairet; Costume Design by Debra Krajec; Light Design by Chester Loeffler-Bell. Performers (L to R): Alexandra Bonesho, Kelsey Lauren, Kirsten Benjamin and Jennifer Mitchell.

Censored on Final Approach
© 2010, Phylis Ravel
Trade Edition, 2013
ISBN 978-1-934962-71-8

*More Great Plays From
Original Works Publishing*

Bea[u]tiful in the Extreme

by Leon Martell

9 or more actors playing multiple roles

Synopsis: America, 1809. Barely in his thirties, Meriwether Lewis, with his friend and partner William Clark, had led an expedition across the continent and back. He was a national hero, the governor of the Louisiana Territory, and he killed himself. Bea[u]tiful in the Extreme, his own words to describe the prairie, follows Meriwether Lewis as he wrestles the demons in his mind. Between the time of his first suicide attempt on a flat boat down the Mississippi, and his final self execution in an inn on the Natchez trace, Lewis relives the triumphs and trials of his epic journey. With Thomas Jefferson, his mentor, Sacagawea the native girl as his guide, and William Clark, his friend, anchor and in many ways soul mate, he struggles to find meaning in all he has seen and done. A warrior faces evil spirits, broken dreams, and politicians in his final battle. Whiskey, meat, laughs, and laudanum on the long trail to immortality.

Liberation

by Steve Patterson

5 Males, 4 Females

Synopsis: Set during the heat of the Bosnian conflict, a young Bosnian soldier deserts his company, fleeing with his sister to a Sarajevo newspaper office in hopes of striking a deal. In exchange for safe passage out of Bosnia, he will give eyewitness testimony of his company's participation in the massacres of Muslim men and boys and systematic rapes of Muslim women. But before his testimony can be recorded, the office is surrounded by Serbian infantry. The newspaper editors are given 24 hours to give up the soldier or be stormed by the troops.

*Contains heavy language and violence.

Censored on Final Approach

By Phylis Ravel

Background of *Censored on Final Approach*

The women who were a part of the Women Airforce Service Pilots program of more than half a century ago wanted merely to serve their country in time of war. To do so, they endured bigotry that was not only routinely demeaning but occasionally fatal. That they also might, years later (as some characters in this play do) choose to forget how their colleagues died and concentrate instead on memories of good times with youthful friends is perhaps natural. The fact is, however, that this play about the American military's first women fliers does not focus on relatively tame late-century sexual problems resembling the Tailhook or Kelly Flinn fiascoes but rather on homicidal sabotage and consequent cover-ups. The result is not a simple good-versus-evil scenario. Instead, *Censored* brings a nearly forgotten history to life as it shows the three-dimensional conflict implied and expressed among the males and females, the non-coms and the officers, the staffers and the pilots and the commanders in the American military (and American society) of 1943-45. WASPs and Other Pilots: Historical Context in *Censored on Final Approach*, Mark D. Noe – War, Literature, and the Arts, An International Journal of the Humanities - Volume 15. Article found online at *http://wlajournal.com/backissues.htm*

Other websites of the WASPs
http://www.wingsacrossamerica.us
https://www.twu.edu/library/wasp.asp

History of the Play

Censored on Final Approach was written in 1993. In 1994 the play premiered at the Women in Theatre Conference at Hofstra University. Since that time, the play has been produced professionally at Alice's Fourth Floor in New York, The Players' Club in New York, Pleiades Theatre in Lexington, Kentucky, the Spangdahlem Air Force Base in Bitburg, Germany and optioned for film by Pachyderm Productions. University productions include Keane College, University of North Dakota, Manatee Community College, Suffolk Community College, Loyola Marymount University in Los Angeles, and Marquette University, University of Wisconsin – Oshkosh, and University of Wisconsin – Parkside. The play has been selected for reading in Women's Studies Program in a number of universities. *Censored on Final Approach* was runner-up for the Jane Chambers playwriting award. I am most grateful to WASPs Madge Rutherford Minton, Nonnie Anderson, Margaret Gilman, Bee Haydu, and Dawn Seymour who extended their friendship and memories. The play is inspired by the stories of Camp Davis. Historical figures are Jacqueline Cochran and Major Stephenson. All other figures are composites of individual stories.

Censored on Final Approach was produced in workshop by Hofstra University's Department of Drama and Dance, Hempstead, New York at the Emily and Jerry Spiegel Theatre November 22, 1993 directed by Phylis Ward Fox with music by Michael DiPaolo, Lighting Design by Megan McClung and Stage Managed by Vanessa Edwards. The cast featured Antoinette Accardi, Jennifer Baker, Jennifer Fox, Jason O'Connell, Cara Pontillo, Rick Suvalle, and Adrienne Thompson*.

On October 7, 1994 ***Censored on Final Approach*** was presented as a mainstage production at Hofstra University's national Women in Theatre Conference at the West End Theatre. It was directed by Phylis Ward Fox with music composed by Michaelangelo DiPaolo, music director, Steven Lavner, set and light design by D.J. Markley, Costume Design by Tim Rucker, flight choreographer Alicia Mikoloski and stage managed by Riham Farid.

The cast was as follows:

Catherine - Lisa Ortiz

The Brother - Robert Casteline

Gerry - Victoria Minardi

Mary - Alicia Mikoloski

Jacqueline Cochran - Adrienne Thompson*

Liz - Season Malan

The Captain - Christopher Daly

The Operations Officer - Seamus Hurley

The Mechanic - Justin Schultz

*Member, Actors Equity Association

Special thanks to Gary Garrison, Stephen Hudson-Mairet, Debra Krajec, Dr. James Kolb, Beth Lincks, David Ravel, Judith Royer, and Peter Sander.

CENSORED ON FINAL APPROACH

Time: The summer of 1943 and 1955

Locations: The home of Catherine Watts in northern California (1955) and various locations at Camp Davis, North Carolina. (1943)

Cast of Characters:

Private First Class Donald Foster - age 25

Catherine Watts - age 25 and 35

Elizabeth Langley – age 22

Gerry Hansen - age 23 and 33

Mary O'Connor – age 20

Jacqueline Cochran - age 37

Major John Stephenson - age 28

Lieutenant Paul Ryder - age 23

Wayne Langhorn - age 39

The Control Tower Operator - age 23*

The Serviceman - age 19*

Artillery Officer - age 23*

Artillery Trainee - age 18*

*These can be double cast

Major Stephenson, Gerry Hansen, and Wayne Langhorn are southerners. Jacqueline Cochran is also from the south; however, she emulated Eleanor Roosevelt when speaking. Her southern dialect would slip in when it suited her.

The flying sequence has the potential of a full theatrical event. Sound, lights, and choreographed movement can play a major role. However, the scene can also work with just the actors and the text.

Special Note: The following words are used by characters in the play: 1) Jap: This term refers to the Japanese. This term reflects a time in history when the United States was at war with Japan. 2) Geronimo: This term refers to the Native American leader and medicine man of the Chiricahua Apache tribe. During World War II, His name was used by the United States military as a warrior cry of victory.

CENSORED ON FINAL APPROACH

Act One

(There are five acting areas with minimal set pieces. Changes of time and location are accomplished through sharp area lighting and sound. The houselights go out. The pre-set remains on. All the actors enter and go to their positions. CATHERINE WATTS, GERRY HANSEN, ELIZABETH (LIZ) LANGLEY, MARY O'CONNOR, JACQUELINE COCHRAN, DONALD FOSTER, WAYNE LANGHORN, LT. PAUL RYDER, ARTILLERY OFFICER and MAJOR JOHN STEPHENSON, are on the stage. The FIVE men and JACQUELINE COCHRAN are on the upstage platforms. Their backs are to the audience. GERRY is upstage slightly left of CATHERINE. CATHERINE sits on the bench downstage right. LIZ and MARY are downstage left. Once the actors are in position, the lights go to black.

MUSIC: ESTABLISHES IN THE BLACK – "In My Solitude" sung by Billy Holiday. The lights come up on CATHERINE, then GERRY. MUSIC goes under and out. The other actors are in shadow. CATHERINE is drinking from a small, delicate, monogrammed silver flask. By the nervous exuberance of GERRY'S first lines, it is obvious that she has been attempting to draw CATHERINE into conversation. The beat change is simply another futile attempt to reach CATHERINE.)

GERRY: No one could out-fly her. Not you -- not me -- not Mary. And the men -- hell, she left them in the dust. *(Silence.)* I saw Don before I came here. He sends his best. *(Silence.)* He said he wrote you. He called you. He... *(CATHERINE takes another swig from her flask. It is painfully apparent CATHERINE wants nothing to do with GERRY.)* I'll let myself out. *(GERRY starts to leave.)*

CATHERINE: You haven't aged.

GERRY: You haven't either.

CATHERINE: Inside. Inside I am old as Methuselah.

GERRY: *(Taking another chance.)* Did you know Don had no idea she signed on?

(Lights up on LIZ and DONALD.)

DONALD: Liz, have you gone squirrely?! We're *suppose* to get married!

LIZ: You said we had to wait out the war. I'm just helping. The faster we win - and you come home - the faster we can have our own baseball team.

DONALD: This is no joke!

LIZ: I never said birthing nine sons was a joke -- although I'm sure we'll have a lot of giggles!

DONALD: Liz, you're not going.

LIZ: We're not married yet, Don. That means you're not my commanding officer. *(Pause.)* I won't be flying combat, darling. Sweetwater, Texas isn't Pearl Harbor. *(Pause. Then very determined.)* Jason would have wanted me to do this.

DONALD: Jason would have put you over his knee and spanked you within an inch of your life. Which is exactly what your father should have done when you first stepped onto a plane.

LIZ: We're military, Don. Dad's given me his blessing. I'd like yours.

DONALD: And if I don't –

LIZ: I'll still love you.

(DONALD takes a moment. He's not sure if he should say what is on his mind. He decides to follow through.)

DONALD: Liz, nothing you do can make up for Jason dying.

LIZ: This has nothing to do with my brother.

DONALD: It has everything to do with your brother.

LIZ: Please, Don -- just say you love me - we'll take care of everything else after the war.

DONALD: Of course, I love you, knucklehead. But after we're married, you will not step on a plane, you hear me?

LIZ: Cross my heart and hope to –

DONALD: Don't say it -- I love you.

LIZ: Why?

DONALD: For God and Country! Love you!

(Lights out on LIZ and DONALD.)

CATHERINE: She was so damned patriotic. Listening to Mary and Liz -- you'd think...

(Lights up on LIZ and MARY.)

LIZ: I saw it! I saw it! I was flying up, up -- and there it was -- a halo all around my plane!

MARY: Oh, yes -- flying right up into the arms of God!

CATHERINE: Arms of God! Did you hear that Miss Hansen?

GERRY: Indeed. Indeed, Miss Watts. But if the truth be known, I have never felt that way when I was flying.

LIZ: Of course you have.

MARY: How could you not?

GERRY: I just haven't.

LIZ: You mean to tell me that flying doesn't ignite something beyond –

GERRY: Oh, it ignites -- the take-off -- when you rev up. And then you feel the vibration right under you. I don't know about you, but I get all soft and warm inside.

LIZ: I wouldn't go that far.

MARY: *(squeals)* I cannot believe you! I cannot believe you! I cannot believe you!

GERRY: Oh, come on now, Mary, you were raised on a farm.

MARY: My folks raised chickens; they reared me.

(LIZ and MARY are obviously embarrassed and, at the same time, intrigued by GERRY'S risqué performance.)

GERRY: Now, where was I? Oh, yes, the take-off -- real slow approach -- vibrations are steady but warm, and then you pick up speed for lift off, but it's a gradual build, and that vibration that you thought was just lovelier than all get out, well, it gets even more intense -- surprise, surprise -- and what with the speed for take-off building, the vibration along with it, before you know it you're feelin' kind-a-damp. Oh, now come on -- don't tell me you haven't experienced... -- even virgins have wet dreams.

LIZ: Cut it out!

(MARY by this time is speechless. CATHERINE is enjoying the fun.)

GERRY: So here I am into the approach for take-off -- speeding along, wheels just barely caressing the pavement. and it's faster, faster, and then you suddenly lift up, and up -- and you feel those flaps going in... under I mean, and the vibration goes deeper -- passed the thighs, passed the -- you want to talk about finding God?

LIZ: Stop it!

MARY: I think that's a good idea.

CATHERINE: No, don't you dare stop!

GERRY: And then you're at this steady flow -- this holier than oh my goodness never-going-to-end -- and I'm going to squeeze every last vibration from every little part of the plane. Then there's this moment -- everything stops -- and you're on top -- so to speak -- you have come into your moment. And then you are -- floating -- perfect visibility for miles -- inside and out. Sometimes, there's even a view.

LIZ: Very nice.

MARY: What's so nice about it?!

CATHERINE: Best thing since hot fudge sundaes.

GERRY: And I'm not done.

CATHERINE: She's not done. She needs the cherry on the whip crème.

MARY: Oh, dear.

LIZ: Oh, yes you are!

(As GERRY continues, LIZ and MARY try and grab GERRY. CATHERINE protects GERRY. GERRY is determined to finish her verbal "flight.")

GERRY: So now, it's time to come down -- and what's nice about coming down is that it's as terrific as coming -- up. So here's final approach.

LIZ: *(Diving for GERRY.)* That's enough. We are fair young maidens. And proud of it.

GERRY: You take a wide swing. Almost as if you're gettin' a second wind.

(MARY squeals.)

LIZ: I'm countin' to three! One!

CATHERINE: That'a girl, Gerry!

LIZ: One and a half!

GERRY: The wide swing does something to your belly!

CATHERINE: Don't you dare stop, Miss Hansen! *(CATHERINE is circling LIZ.)* Touch her, and we'll chop you up for firewood!

GERRY: You finish that wide swing and start the approach –

LIZ: Two!

GERRY: The speed increases -- building... You feel flaps opening.

LIZ: Two and a half. Gerryyyyyy!

MARY: Don't say it! Don't say it!

CATHERINE: Building... Building... Keep going! I can feel those flaps!

GERRY: The wheels drop! Speed makes –

CATHERINE: Wheels drop! Wow! Contact!

LIZ: Two and three quarters! I'm warning you!

MARY: You are naughty! Naughty! Naughty! We don't talk that way!

GERRY/CATHERINE: ...contact with wheels -- contact with ground.

CATHERINE: And what do you know, but here's that ol'devil vibration...

LIZ: And Two and three quarters and... Last chance!

GERRY: But this time he's coming for his due. It hits!

LIZ/MARY: Three!

GERRY: Pull on the brakes!

(They tickle each other - screaming and laughing uncontrollably.)

MARY: I'm gonna have to go to confession! Hey, don't mess up my dress!

LIZ: Prepare to meet your maker!

GERRY/CATHERINE: And slide! Slide! Slide!

(GERRY and CATHERINE tickle LIZ and MARY senseless. The laughter subsides as the lights change. SOUND: Laughter of the WOMEN up and under as the scene changes. LIZ and MARY slowly leave the lighted area, as GERRY and CATHERINE continue.)

GERRY: Those were good times. *(Silence.)* Why didn't you talk to Don?

CATHERINE: There was nothing to say.

GERRY: Every year he writes you.

CATHERINE: I don't read his letters.

GERRY: And mine?

CATHERINE: You're here, aren't you?

GERRY: He wants to know what happened.

CATHERINE: Liz died on final approach.

GERRY: He knows that. He wants to know why. I want to know why.

(Lights up on LT. RYDER.)

LT. RYDER: It was an accident. Pilot error.

(Lights down on LT. RYDER.)

CATHERINE: Too bad you didn't stick around.

GERRY: Guilty! All right?! I don't know how many ways I can apologize.

CATHERINE: There are casualties in war.

(Lights up on the ARTILLERY OFFICER.)

ARTILLERY OFFICER: That's our second casualty, Lieutenant. Decisions have to be made.

(Lights down on the ARTILLERY OFFICER.)

GERRY: You're talking about Liz -- not some damned statistic!

(Lights up on MAJOR STEPHENSON.)

MAJOR STEPHENSON: Miss Watts, I am not at liberty to speak to you.

(Lights down on MAJOR STEPHENSON.)

GERRY: I can't believe it was pilot error.

CATHERINE: I'm sure Don showed you the accident report.

GERRY: Censored. A whole paragraph cut out.

(Lights up on WAYNE.)

WAYNE: The lady was a top flyer. The plane wasn't. I'll swear that on a stack of Bibles.

(Lights down on WAYNE.)

CATHERINE: So?

GERRY: You can't tell me her death meant nothing to you.

CATHERINE: Gerry, it's over. The war ended, and so did we. *(Drinking from her flask.)* I'd offer you one but I prefer to drink alone.

GERRY: I don't drink anymore.

CATHERINE: Too bad. One of the two things you did well.

GERRY: Don't do that anymore either.

CATHERINE: You weren't at the funeral.

GERRY: That was ten years ago.

CATHERINE: Well, like an elephant.

GERRY: I'm sorry I disappointed you.

CATHERINE: Do us both a favor. Leave. Now.

GERRY: Not till I have the answers.

CATHERINE: I stopped asking questions.

GERRY: It's time people knew.

CATHERINE: Knew what? That women flew planes for the military? That some made it and some didn't.

GERRY: You know damn well what I mean. *(Pause.)* Don't you want people to know the truth?

CATHERINE: You think I know the truth?

GERRY: You know more than I do. I've been to Washington, Sweetwater, Camp Davis. It's as if we never existed.

CATHERINE: Well, I'm not about to rip myself apart so you can feel better.

GERRY: Fine. OK. Fine. You don't care about me and I don't care about you. I think we can live with that. I want to know how and why she died, so I can make peace with myself, and maybe set the record straight. And if you think that's selfish, tough.   (continued)

GERRY (Cont'd): Jesus, Catherine -- We went through a hell of a lot together. And if I could do it all over again I would! Right now! Damnit. You were there! You saw the report before it was censored. What was on the report? You owe this to Liz!

CATHERINE: Don't you dare presume to know what I owe Liz!

GERRY: I'm sorry. I'm sorry. *(Starts to leave.)* This was a bad idea.

(GERRY gathers her purse and gloves. She can't get out fast enough.)

CATHERINE: *(After a moment.)* I have something for you.

(She takes a hankie out of her pocket and unfolds it. She holds the open hankie out to GERRY.)

GERRY: *(She takes from the hankie a small pin shaped like wings.)* My wings.

CATHERINE: The last time we were together you…

GERRY: Thank you.

CATHERINE: I don't know why I kept them.

GERRY: I'm glad you did.

CATHERINE: You sure you don't want a drink?

GERRY: That stuff will kill you.

CATHERINE: I hope. *(Pause.)* There's nothing to tell. It's over. I want it to be over. We were just an experiment, Gerry. An experiment –

(*Lights up on JACQUELINE COCHRAN.*)

JACQUELINE: Once you accept this assignment, there is no turning back. You are sworn to secrecy.

(*Lights down on JACQUELINE COCHRAN.*)

CATHERINE: "Sworn to secrecy." -- an experiment for the Army.

GERRY: How is Miss Cochran?

CATHERINE: She moved on. Like we all did.

GERRY: I read she was the first American woman to fly into Hiroshima after the war. She said it was hard landing 'cause of the weather -- poor visibility for miles. Pissed her off.

GERRY: *(Pause.)* Do you still have your wings?

CATHERINE: As a matter of fact -- *(Taking the wings out of her her pocket.)*

GERRY: Cochran's wings –

(*The light comes up on MARY and ELIZABETH.*)

MARY: They are gorgeous. I wish I could get more -- I'd send them to my sisters.

LIZ: You earned those wings, Miss Mary. It's not a souvenir.

MARY: I cannot believe it! I cannot believe it! I cannot believe it!

CATHERINE: I am not going to ask her what she can't believe.

MARY: A reception with Miss Jacqueline Cochran at the Mayflower Hotel -- have you ever seen such plush furniture? And we're treated like we're important. And the Dodge Hotel right on Capitol Hill - the rooms have hot and cold running water. The bed is enormous and soft, and I can order all the ice cream I want just by calling the operator! Its Christmas morning!

GERRY: Well, enjoy it -- because you'll be in two by four bunks in forty-eight hours and K-rations.

MARY: Oh, I don't care. I'm the first member of my family that's going to see the White House.

LIZ: There she is! There's our Miss Cochran!

GERRY: Don't genuflect. She's only a woman.

LIZ: That's not just any woman. *That* woman is the reason why we are flying!

CATHERINE: You're right, Liz. If it weren't for her -- it would just be the debutantes.

LIZ: And you're our only debutante!

MARY: Miss Cochran! Miss Cochran!

(There is the sound of 25 females applauding. LIZ, MARY, and CATHERINE lead the ovation. GERRY is courteous but reserved. As this scene takes place -- CATHERINE and GERRY are downstage right; LIZ and MARY are downstage left. JACQUELINE is center.)

JACQUELINE: Thank you. Thank you. Thank you. *(beat.)* You all look beautiful. I cannot express to you what is stirring in my heart. I look at your faces -- and I thank God that He has seen fit to use me -- to use us all. When I was no bigger than a grasshopper, I used to go to a small little church in my small little town -- and there was this preacher, and he would lift up his voice and we would all join in singin' God's praises. *(JACQUELINE starts to recite the words.)* "Dwellin' in Beulah Land!" I'm feeling that as a woman who can serve my country I am dwellin' in Beulah Land. I am living on that mountain. I am living one of the greatest moments in our history as a nation. And it is my highest honor to share that moment of history with you. Your program of training has equipped you to fulfill any noncombatant flying assignments reserved for men. We will take over their burdens so as to free our men for combat service. Each and every one of you has been carefully chosen for this mission. And it is a mission – A top-secret mission. You are doing more than ferrying planes up and down the coast. I am not belittlin' that type of work the WAFS have been assigned. Lord knows, I led a group of American women pilots to assist the British Air Transport Auxiliary in ferrying operational equipment long before Colonel Tunner and Nancy Love instituted their program. You ladies are about to serve your country in a way no other women in our history have ever done. You are the first non-ferrying group of women pilots. You will be towing targets for artillery trainees. Tow target pilots. High altitude precision flying. You are the first women given this assignment. You will not be the last. As you dedicate yourself to this mission know that President and Mrs. Roosevelt offer their deepest respect for your courage and selflessness. President Roosevelt speaks of every American's rendezvous with destiny. I am sure when he spoke those words he was not thinking only of American men but the women who serve -- and those women are you. And now, Ladies, I have a plane to fly. And so do you! *(Applause. JACKIE begins to leave and sees CATHERINE. She goes to CATHERINE and takes her aside.)* Why, dear Miss Watts, I am so pleased you are flyin' with us.

CATHERINE: So am I.

MARY: *(Whispers to LIZ and GERRY.)* Did you know Catherine knew her?

CATHERINE: *(Privately to JACQELINE.)* Is Miss Love a little upset with me?

JACQUELINE: *(Privately to CATHERINE.)* Not as upset with you as she is with me.

CATHERINE: I'm sorry.

JACQUELINE: Thank you, Miss Watts. I have pretty thick skin. But I can't do this without my women. I'll be depending on you at Camp Davis. Keep by my side. *(Speaking to the others.)* I was telling Miss Watts that I'll be depending on all of you to move this mission forward.

MARY: We'll make you proud, Miss Cochran.

JACQUELINE: *(Wanting to move on to the next appointment.)* Well, God Bless you all. Fly high, fly straight, and have a smooth landing.

(*JACQUELINE starts to leave.*)

LIZ: Miss Cochran, there are rumors that we will soon be militarized.

JACQUELINE: Not exactly rumors, Miss...

CATHERINE: *(Whispering to JACQUELINE.)* Langley - her brother, Corporal Jason Langley, died at Pearl Harbor. Her Father - career man – Army – master sergeant.

JACQUELINE: Miss Langley. There are discussions but nothing is official yet. As you may or may not know, as of last week, I am in charge of the women pilots in the Army Air Forces and while we are not militarized, we have a name. Each of you serves our country as a WASP. You are part of The Women Air Force Service Pilots. And while you are not military, you do have all the rights of the officers, and you don't have to salute *(Pause.)* That was a little "itty bitty" joke.

(The WOMEN laugh.)

JACQUELINE (Cont'd): Most important, as civilians you are not obligated to take any assignment to which you feel you are not suited.

GERRY: Why is that so important?

JACQUELINE: Well, right now, this whole business of women flying is touch and go. It's a little difficult for our men to conceive of us flying -- much less flying with military status. You might meet up with some hostile CO who wants to put you through the wringer. Well, as a civilian, he has to think twice about the demands he puts on you. You know the military, Miss-

LIZ/CATHARINE: Langley.

JACQUELINE: What do they say? "Don't think! Just follow orders!"

LIZ: Oh, I know that ma'am. I'm an army brat.

JACQUELINE: Now, I remember -- Your dear brother, Corporal Jason Langley, gave his life for his country -- Pearl Harbor.

LIZ: *(Greatly moved that she knows her brother's name.)* Yes, ma'am. Thank you, ma'am.

JACQUELINE: And your father. Career man -- Master Sergeant. Now, they're the men who really run the army.

LIZ: *(Even more impressed.)* Yes, ma'am.

JACQUELINE: Yes, I do. *(To all the women.)* I know some of you want to be military –

GERRY: Not me!

LIZ: Shush!

JACQUELINE: At present you are better off with civilian status. That includes me -- now, don't you think I'd like Colonel in front of my name? We all have to patiently wait. And if there's one thing women can do well, is wait.

LIZ: Miss Cochran, if we are not military, what are we to the military?

JACQUELINE: Something special. Chosen. We're here to serve. We are here to win this war. Ladies, take the challenge. *(To Liz.)* Must be difficult for a military child to grasp this whole civilian balance -- just as hard, I guess, as it is for the men to even consider us ladies piloting planes.

LIZ: I meant no disrespect, Miss Cochran. Whatever you have in store for us, I want it.

JACQUELINE: Just to serve your country.

GERRY: For God, country, and the thrill of it?

MARY: *(Under her breath.)* Gerry.

JACQUELINE: …Most certainly not for the thrill of it.

CATHERINE: She didn't mean it the way it sounded.

GERRY: Oh, no, ma'am. Military or civilian -- what difference does it make?! We're doing what no other women have been able to do.

MARY: That's right. And I, for one, want to thank you for that - from the bottom of my heart.

JACQUELINE: No need to thank me. Just do your job. That and that alone is thanks enough. *(To everyone but particularly to LIZ.)* And I can assure you that I want my women part of the armed forces. I will fight for that. That is a promise.

CATHERINE: *(Wanting to change the subject - with fake seriousness.)* There is one *problem*, Miss Cochran.

JACQUELINE: Yes, Miss Watts.

CATHERINE: A rather delicate problem-

JACQUELINE: Yes.

CATHERINE: Uniforms.

JACQUELINE: Well, that's a question I like to answer. When you get to Camp Davis, you do have new flight uniforms, and they have assured me they will do their utmost to form fit them for you. However, next month I am havin' a fashion show for General Arnold. I'll be showing him three styles, and if I play my cards right, you will have the most stylish uniforms ever worn in the military. Niemann Marcus issued. Well, if I can't get Niemann Marcus, Bergdorf Goodman will just have to do. Ladies, I have a plane to fly and so do you. Your flight leaves 0600 tomorrow. God Bless you. Oh, before I forget. You can tell the other girls that you'll all be receiving a sample of my new cosmetics, "Wings for Beauty". I've developed a new colorless lipstick I made for husband Floyd. He's got the worst dry lips -- but it works good when you're flying those high altitudes. *(JACQUELINE says the next line in dead earnest, as if the outcome of the war depended on it.)* I hope you ladies remember that no matter how long, or how tough your assignment is, when you land, you do not leave that plane, until you have combed your hair and touched up your make-up.

GERRY: Yes, ma'am.

MARY: *(Whispers to LIZ.)* But I don't wear make-up.

JACQUELINE: And one other very important matter – a s a WASP you are expected to behave as if you were officers. Do not date the enlisted men. And, if I were you, I would not date the officers for a few weeks; and when you do, sweet Lord, use your discretion.

MARY: We will! We will! Except for Miss Langley! She's engaged.

JACQUELINE: And now, ladies, I have a plane to fly! Now, top of your lungs -- let's hear it! *(JACQUELINE starts singing to the tune of "Yankee Doodle Dandy" and everyone joins in.)* We are Yankee Doodle, Pilots...

THE WOMEN: Yankee Doodle Do or Die, Real live nieces of our Uncle Sam, Born with a yearning to fly, Keep to step to all our classes, March to flight line with our pals, Yankee Doodle came to Texas, Just to fly the *PT*'s, We are those Yankee Doodle gals.

(As they begin singing "Real live nieces of our Uncle Sam", a snare drum takes up the beat and follows throughout the next scenes as indicated. When the ladies reach "Keep to step to all our classes", they begin to march off, as JACQUELINE waves good-bye. Simultaneously, the men set up the ready room. A telephone is handed to JACQUELINE.)

JACQUELINE: General Hap Arnold. Miss Cochran returning his call. General Arnold, I wanted to get back to you sooner, but I was saying good-bye to my girls. I'm so proud of them, sir. They will prove their worth to the military. I guarantee you that. They are heading for Camp Davis as we speak!   (continued)

JACQUELINE (Cont'd): They are ready. They are willing. They are able. Pardon me! *(A little irritated.)* Well, of course, Camp Davis is ready for them!

(Drum riff. JACQUELINE exits. Drum riff. ARTILLERY OFFICER ENTERS with the ARTILLERY TRAINEE running towards him from the other side of the stage.)

ARTILLERY TRAINEE: Permission to speak, sir!

ARTILLERY OFFICER: At ease soldier.

ARTILLERY TRAINEE: Is it true, Sir?

ARTILLERY OFFICER: Don't ask questions unless you know the answers.

ARTILLERY TRAINEE: Yes, sir. I know the answer, sir.

ARTILLERY OFFICER: And the answer?

ARTILLERY OFFICER: The ladies cannot date enlisted men.

ARTILLERY OFFICER: And…

ARTILLERY TRAINEE: I am an enlisted man. That said, sir, you are an officer, sir. I would be honored to chauffeur you and your special guest to any location.

ARTILLERY OFFICER: Soldier. I am very married. Two small children, and a beautiful wife, I might add. *(ARTILLERY OFFICER starts to leave.)*

ARTILLERY TRAINEE: How long will it take me to become an officer?

ARTILLERY OFFICER: God willing, the war will be over.

(Drum riff. ARTILLERY OFFICER and ARTILLERY TRAINEE exit. Drum riff. LT. RYDER marches to center stage holding a large army issued box. MAJOR STEPHENSON comes from stage left holding a clip board with inventory sheets and a pencil.)

LT. RYDER: Major, sir.

MAJOR STEPHENSON: Yes, Mister.

LT. RYDER: *(Amused.)* There's been a mistake, sir - in the supply room, sir. Sergeant asked me to bring this over.

MAJOR STEPHENSON: Is it contraband?

LT. RYDER: Not exactly, sir.

(LT. RYDER lifts from the box, a white cotton brassiere. There is no response.)

MAJOR STEPHENSON: Return it to supplies, Mister. They will be issued 0900 tomorrow.

LT. RYDER: Sir?!

MAJOR STEPHENSON: Tell the sergeant these with the other supplies arriving at 1500 today. *(He rapidly reads off the list.)* Ersatz bobbie pins, hairnets, shower caps, undergarments, including slips and elastic garters *(and barely audible) and... (he reads items but says instead...)* other feminine hygiene items of a personal nature.

LT. RYDER: You mean, there are going to be wo –

MAJOR STEPHENSON: Yes, Mister. Female flyers. *(LT. RYDER starts to laugh.)* Top Secret! *(LT. RYDER stops in mid-laugh.)* Dismissed!

(LT. RYDER, laughing, makes an about face and marches up center and exits. Drum riff accompanies his exit. At the same moment a uniformed non-com wheels out a clothes rack where four uniforms are hanging along with boots, belts, and socks. WAYNE shakes his head and exits. MAJOR STEPHENSON looks at the clothes rack specified for the female flyers and remarks:)

MAJOR STEPHENSON: Dear God, get this war over before the whole nation goes berserk.

(The snare drum underlines MAJOR STEPHENSON'S exit stage left. The YOUNG WOMEN, dressed in their underwear, march on stage right singing.)

LIZ/MARY/GERRY/CATHERINE: We are Yankee Doodle Pilots, Yankee Doodle Do or Die –

(The singing comes to an abrupt stop as the young women see the flight uniforms and shoes issued to them.)

GERRY: Oh, shoot, they've given us men's flight suits again. Oh, shoot.

CATHERINE: I don't think they want us to entice the men.

LIZ: Well, at least our undergarments were the right size.

GERRY: That's because we ordered them! What the hell happened to Niemann Marcus!

LIZ: Okay. Shoes... for you... no. Those are mine. Here. Take these.

MARY: I guess they weren't expecting us. What's all these pockets for?

GERRY: Flashlight, of course, if you're smart, you'll squeeze a lipstick in there. You're latest penguin book -- romance, of course, your compact case, and don't break that mirror, or you'll have seven years bad luck -- marriageable years, I might add. A screwdriver and perfume -- Evening in Paris or Chanel, extra underwear for when we can't get back to base and ... what the heck are these zippers for? *(The front zipper has two openings. One zipper is at the top and one is at the bottom. GERRY works both zippers and remarks.)* The bottom one's non-applicable, ladies. Well, let's get crackin' -- we got to put some style in these godforsaken clothes.

(As they are putting on their clothes, when they are not talking, they are singing "Yankee Doodle Gals" – just playing around.)

CATHERINE: Pull it a little tighter.

GERRY: I'll love pulling outfits tighter. Here I go. Tighter. Tighter. There.

CATHERINE: Now, we're starting to look like women of fashion.

MARY: You think so?

GERRY: She doesn't understand irony.

CATHERINE: Ouch! You trying to kill me before the war's over?

GERRY: Sorry. I didn't know there was flesh there.

CATHERINE: Hour-glass figures are not in fashion.

GERRY: Says who?

CATHERINE: Says anyone who doesn't have an hour-glass figure.

MARY: How do I look?

CATHERINE: Like Rebecca of Sunnybrook Farm.

MARY: Thank you.

LT. RYDER: *(over loudspeaker)* Ladies, report to ready room on the double.

MARY: My Gosh! That's it! Here we go!

GERRY: Hold your horses, Mary -- let me finish tiein' my boots.

MARY: Well, hurry.

CATHERINE: Slow down, Mary. The war's still going to be there.

MARY: I just want to show them we're right on schedule.

LIZ: We'll show them! Don't worry!

(The girls move swiftly to the acting area - ready room.)

CATHERINE: Watts reporting, sir.

LIZ: Langley, reporting, sir.

MARY: O'Connor, reporting, sir.

GERRY: Hansen, reporting, sir.

LT. RYDER: I believe a salute is in order.

LIZ: We're civilians, sir. However, we look forward to the day that we can salute you, sir.

LT: RYDER. I cannot say the same, ma'am. Your orders are as follows –

LIZ: Yes, sir.

CATHERINE: Yes, sir.

MARY: Yes, sir.

GERRY: Yes, sir.

LT. RYDER: Ladies. You must allow me to issue your orders before answering in the affirmative. However, I do appreciate your willingness. Availability on the part of a young woman is something I truly appreciate. *(The double meaning does not go unnoticed by the women.)* Now, you are assigned L-5's -- your mission is administrative and tracking flights. You will fly low altitude missions -- takin' it slow -- you are to take radioed orders from ground station Sugar Charley.

LIZ: Sir. Are you referring to the gun crew that shoot camera film?

LT. RYDER: Affirmative.

LIZ: Sir. We have been assigned to tow targets. Live ammunition, sir.

LT. RYDER: Those aren't the orders, ma'am.

CATHERINE: There must be some error.

LT. RYDER: Oh, yes, ma'am. There is an error.

MARY: If you could just point us in the direction, sir –

LIZ: One minute, Mary. *(To LT. RYDER.)* I'd like to speak with the CO.

LT. RYDER: He's fightin' a war ma'am. These are your orders. You're civilians. Take them or leave them. *(LT. RYDER exits.)*

CATHERINE: *(Not so LT. RYDER can hear.)* Oh, we'll take them all right, but you can bet your sweet stripes, Lieutenant, you won't hear the last of it. *(CATHERINE turns to the other WOMEN.)* Excuse me, ladies; I have to talk to the horse's mouth.

(As they exit, lights immediately up on two acting areas. MAJOR STEPHENSON and LT. RYDER are in one area. JACQUELINE is in another. JACQUELINE and LT. RYDER are speaking to each other on telephones. MAJOR STEPHENSON is doing the paper work. The ARTILLERY OFFICER is working with MAJOR STEPHENSON.)

MAJOR STEPHENSON: That woman again? If she calls one more time I'll have her girls cleaning out latrines. *(LT. RYDER nods.)* Carry on, Lieutenant.

ARTILLERY OFFICER: Major – the women are scheduled to fly at 0800.

MAJOR STEPHENSON: Like hell they are.

ARTILLERY OFFICER: We have one war, sir. We don't need another.

LT. RYDER: He is unavailable, Miss Cochran.

JACQUELINE: Oh, is he now? Well, please inform Major Stephenson that General Arnold is standing beside me and would like to know precisely when Major Stephenson will become available.

LT. RYDER: May I repeat that, ma'am?

JACQUELINE: Repeat, whatever, you like.

LT. RYDER: You are sayin' that General Hap Arnold is standing beside you and would like to know precisely when Major Stephenson will become available.

ARTILLERY OFFICER: Major, perhaps –

MAJOR STEPHENSON: *(As he goes over to the phone, he hands the orders to the ARTILLERY OFFICER.)* Here are your orders.

ARTILLERY OFFICER: Permission to speak, sir.

MAJOR STEPHENSON: Your orders. Now.

(ARTILLERY OFFICER takes the orders and exits.)

LT. RYDER: Pardon me, ma'am, but he has just come through the door.

JACQUELINE: Thank you, Lieutenant.

(As MAJOR STEPHENSON talks with JACQUELINE COCHRAN, he is signing papers handed to him by LT. RYDER: As the conversation continues the activity stops as he listens -- his response is a slow burn.)

MAJOR STEPHENSON: Miss Cochran.

JACQUELINE: Major Stephenson, thank you so much for taking my call.

MAJOR STEPHENSON: A pleasure, ma'am.

JACQUELINE: I understand there has been some misunderstanding as to the assignments for my women.

MAJOR STEPHENSON: No, misunderstanding, whatsoever, Miss Cochran. They are simply following the prescribed orders for any new cadet assigned to tow targets.

JACQUELINE: The men cadets go directly to the heavier planes. They don't fly cubstuff. Also, my girls have informed me they are denied milk and clean sheets.

MAJOR STEPHENSON: There's a war on ma'am. We are rationed. We did not expect your girls, and supplies were not ordered.

JACQUELINE: Major Stephenson, you're from the south.

MAJOR STEPHENSON: Ma'am..

JACQUELINE: Southerners like stories.

MAJOR STEPHENSON: Ma'am...

JACQUELINE: I know I do.

MAJOR STEPHENSON: Ma'am. I have a meetin' I must attend. Immediately.

JACQUELINE: *(As if she is speaking to General Arnold.)* What did you say, General? You want to hear this story? *(Into the phone.)* General Arnold wants to hear the story, Major Stephenson. I hope you will indulge my female nonsense.

MAJOR STEPHENSON: Yes, ma'am.

JACQUELINE: The story's about when I was a little boy.

MAJOR STEPHENSON: Excuse me, ma'am?

JACQUELINE: When I was a little boy. Well, as you may or may not know. There was a time when we were all little boys. But I am talking about when I was a little boy. When I was a little boy I lived on what's known as "the other side of the tracks" meaning I was dirt poor. And bein' dirt poor I used to stand in front of the General Store in town wishin' I had money to go into the store and buy something. Well, there I was, standing in front of the store when this big ole' Indian came by. He spied me. I spied him. Then he raised-up his big ol' bow and arrow, aimed, fired and shot me right in my gut creating my belly button! Well! I was so shocked; I was so mortified that I sat down on a stump not realizing that there was an axe on it. So that when I sat down, the axe chopped off my "who-who"! And that's how I got to be a little girl! *(MAJOR STEPHENSON is stone silent.)* Are you there, Major?

MAJOR STEPHENSON: Yes, ma'am.

JACQUELINE: Now, I do have a purpose in telling you this story. One should never tell a story unless one has a purpose. You bein' a little boy and me being a little girl is an accident. Like that old axe that chopped of my –

MAJOR STEPHENSON: Yes, ma'am.

JACQUELINE: Now, you know and I know that I am as good or better a pilot than any of your men. You ask Chuck Yeager. And my girls are the same. It's just an accident that they are made of sugar and spice, and you are made of snails and puppy dog tails. Now, I told a little fib. General Arnold is not really here with me. But I am saying as sweetly as my southern tongue can manage that you either put my women on tow targets immediately, or I will truly speak with General Arnold. And I will speak my mind. Now if you'll excuse me, I've got a plane to fly. *(JACQUELINE exits.)*

MAJOR STEPHENSON: Lieutenant. Those women are to be given every shit assignment you can find. And if you run out of things to do, let them sit on their firm little derrieres. One more thing. If the supplies of milk and clean sheets arrive, you give them to our men. I will not have some ex-beauty parlor operator, home wrecker turned pilot tell me how to run a war. Chuck Yeager, my ass.

(Lights up in ready room. MARY is seated alone – reading a letter from home. LIZ and CATHERINE are each reading an operation manual and are seated in a corner away from LT. RYDER. MAJOR STEPHENSON enters.)

LIZ: Major Stephenson, permission to speak, sir.

MAJOR STEPHENSON: Not now, mister... miss... ma'm... you -

(MAJOR STEPHENSON hurriedly exits.)

LIZ: But...

LT. RYDER: He's fightin' a war ma'am. There's a recent copy of *Ladies Home Journal*. You might want to do some catch-up.

MARY: *(Picking up the magazine.)* Thank you.

LIZ: Yes, indeed. Thanks a whole lot.

CATHERINE: I am going out of my mind. *(She takes her flask out.)* God! Could I go for a drink.

LIZ: Catherine! *(CATHERINE motions LIZ over to the far side of the ready room.)* If you get caught-

CATHERINE: I never get caught. It's vodka -- there's no smell.

LIZ: Straight?

CATHERINE: A pony. It's called a pony. Lady, for any army brat, you are real delicate.

LIZ: Sorry. This is the first time I've spent anytime with a blue-blood.

CATHERINE: *(She mimics her mother.)* I hate to disappoint you but *mumsy* considers me tainted. They are not talking to me.

LIZ: Maybe when the war's over, and they see what you've done for you country.

CATHERINE: The only way I'll be *worthy to represent our family* is to quit flying. As a hobby, it's acceptable -- something any husband, of our sort, you understand, would find terribly amusing and just this side of naughty. (cont.)

CATHERINE (Cont'd): Something to tell the boys. Great, just what I need. My flying make some fatuous, old fart a stud!

LIZ: *(Shocked by Catherine's words.)* Do your parents know you talk like this?

CATHERINE: *(Laughing gently at the memory.)* Oh yeah. Dinners were vicious. But I digress. My point, old girl, where is my point -- yes, my point is I will never stop flying. I will fly because that's what I want to do. That's all I've ever wanted to do. I want to die flying the biggest, fastest, slickest plane ever built. And - *(Toasting her mother with the bottle.)* sorry mums, I will die single. *(CATHERINE offers bottle to LIZ.)* Sure you don't want some?

LIZ: You're spiffed. What if they want us to fly?

CATHERINE: Fly? *(She chuckles and takes another sip.)* Besides I never get spiffed. The stuff is like mother's milk to me.

LIZ: What about Miss Cochran? We're her girls. What if you are caught? She's the one who gets in trouble -- the whole program could go down the drain just because of –

CATHERINE: *(Putting the flask away.)* Okay -- you said the magic words. I wouldn't do anything to mess this up for Jackie -- from now on I'll keep this stuff under the barracks.

GERRY: *(Enters.)* What the hell is goin' on here?

LT. RYDER: Excuse me, ma'am?

GERRY. You heard me. I just came back from deliverin' a turkey to some General's wife in some godforsaken little town down the coast.

LT. RYDER: That was your assignment.

GERRY: I'm not in the mood for games, Lieutenant.

LT. RYDER: You are mighty pretty when you are angry, ma'am.

GERRY: Yes. I know.

LT. RYDER: *(LT. RYDER waves a slip of paper in front of Gerry.)* Miss Hansen, do you know what I have here?

GERRY: More turkey deliveries?

LT. RYDER: Better. Your chance to fly for God, Country and the thrill of it.

GERRY: Do you mean a real assignment?

LT. RYDER: Want it?

GERRY: We all want it.

LT. RYDER: I only have one. Think I should hold an auction? Or let it be our little secret.

GERRY: There's only one assignment, and you want to give it to me?

LT. RYDER: I certainly do.

GERRY: Well, hand it over.

LT. RYDER: Now -- now. Not too fast - a little negotiation here.

GERRY: I see.

LT. RYDER: Do you, Miss Hansen?

GERRY: *(GERRY goes to attention. Her movement is military precision.)* Oh, indeed I do. May I see the order?

LT. RYDER: Come a little closer. *(GERRY marches to him.)* Just a little bit more. *(GERRY marches closer and stands at attention facing out.)* I love a young woman who knows how to play. *(LT. RYDER walks behind her and holds the clipboard with the orders so GERRY can read it but not touch it.)* How's that for an assignment?

GERRY: It is a wonderful assignment.

LT. RYDER: And there's only one.

GERRY: I'll take it. *(GERRY tries to take it.)*

LT. RYDER: *(Whipping the paper behind his back.)* And you can report back to me right after the assignment. 2100 behind the hangar, so you can tell me all about it.

GERRY: Is that what you want me to do?

LT. RYDER: I would be honored if you would follow these orders.

GERRY: So there's a string attached.

LT. RYDER: You want to fly, don't you? Somethn' bigger? Better? Here's your chance.

GERRY: You know I do. We all do.

LT. RYDER: My concern. My deep concern revolves around you, Miss Hansen. Here. You can touch it. *(LT. RYDER hands the paper to Gerry.)*

GERRY: *(She runs her hand over the paper but does not touch it.)* My -- this has such a smooth surface.

LT. RYDER: You cannot imagine how smooth, ma'am.

GERRY: You know I love to fly. It's my life.

LT. RYDER: I certainly can understand that.

GERRY: I also like men.

LT. RYDER: I certainly can appreciate that.

GERRY: But I've always managed to have both on my terms. And while flying is something I will never give up; you are definitely something of which I will never, never take up. *(GERRY crumples the paper and throws it at his feet.)*

LT. RYDER: *(He picks up the paper.)* Well, that may cost you in the long run. *(She turns to leave.)* I just have one question. If you were to change your mind how much do you charge, my soiled little dove?

GERRY: *(She takes a moment and smiles.)* I am not a soiled little dove, Lieutenant. I am a falcon. A Kestrel Falcon – the smallest of the falcons. Did you know that falcons were jet fliers of the sky? We have keen vision, and we can hover over our prey. Did you know that unlike other falcons we attack with our beak, not our talons. I am sure, you know nothin' of falcons. So I will demonstrate. *(She pounces)* You son-of-a-reptile! I will tear your eyes out!

(GERRY dives for LT. RYDER. GERRY attacks LT. RYDER. There is a tussle. LIZ, MARY, and CATHERINE grab GERRY before she claws him.)

LT. RYDER: Hold on, lady!

LIZ: Whoa!

CATHERINE: Jesus, Gerry!

MARY: Oh, my God!

GERRY: How dare you presume I am a lady of the night.

LIZ: Don't ruin it for us!

LT. RYDER: I'm calling the Major.

CATHERINE: That's won't be necessary. Let's just drop it.

LIZ: Get over here, Gerry!

MARY: Did he hurt you?

LT. RYDER: Did I hurt her?! She's the one with the goddamn nails!

MAJOR STEPHENSON: *(Off-stage.)* Lieutenant! Office! Now!

CATHERINE: Enough.

(LT. RYDER exits.)

LIZ: What did he say to you?

GERRY: He asked me how much I charged.

MARY: For what?

GERRY: Oh, never mind.

LIZ: That bonehcad. You can't let it get to you.

GERRY: I wouldn't if I could just have a few assignments.

CATHERINE: Cochran's working on it.

GERRY: Like hell, she's working on it. She flew in here – dressed in her new Neiman Marcus uniform. Major Stephenson took off. Decided to check on the trainees out at the artillery sights.

LIZ: Cochran has talked with him. Maybe not that day

GERRY: Maybe not at all. Maybe by carrier pigeon. He doesn't consider her his equal. He's ignoring her.

MARY: He's really ignoring all of us. I think he's shy.

GERRY: He's not shy. He doesn't want us here.

LIZ: We can't do anything. We are under military rules. Cochran talks to Major Stephenson.

GERRY: We're civilians.

LIZ: Under military rules.

GERRY: Which we can ignore at any time.

CATHERINE: Not if we want to fly. Look, Gerry, Major Stephenson is not having an easy time. The men aren't happy we're here.

GERRY: Are you saying that if his men were okay, we'd be flying?

CATHERINE: I'm saying give it more time.

GERRY: More time?

CATHERINE: I think that's what I said.

GERRY: How much more?

CATHERINE: *(To LIZ)* You're the military expert -- how much more time?

LIZ: I'm not a military expert!

CATHERINE: A couple of days? A week? A month? A lifetime?

LIZ: *(Pulling a number for her head)* Seven days – a week – yes. A week.

GERRY: I've got to spend a week with the G.D.O. ogling me?

CATHERINE: Gerry, since when didn't you like men ogling you?

GERRY: I like to pick and choose. Okay. A week. Just keep that gorilla away from me.

(*During the next sequence the following action occurs: 1) A drum riff begins and the WOMEN march into formation. 2) As they march into formation, LT. RYDER marches in and stands at attention. 3) The drum riff ends.*)

LT. RYDER: Bridges, Sloane, Read, and Nevelson report.

CATHERINE: No one else?

LT. RYDE: Yes, ma'am. You ladies are to report to ground school classes. Brush-up.

LIZ: What?!

LT. RYDER: Major's orders! Bridges, Sloane, Read, and Nevelson, move those parachutes!

(*Snare drum riff; the WOMEN march to another lineup, while LT. RYDER makes an about face and faces forward.*)

LT. RYDER: Bridges, Sloane, Reade and Nevelson! Report! (*LT. RYDER hands the WOMEN their orders.*) Ladies.

GERRY: What the hell is going on here?!

LT. RYDER: These are your orders.

LIZ: I'm losing my humor.

CATHERINE: I lost that weeks ago.

MARY: We're spending the day taking down an engine! But that's basic!

LT. RYDER: Bridges, Sloane, Reade and Nevelson! Report Now!

(Snare drum riff. The WOMEN march into a different formation. The MAJOR enters to speak with LT. RYDER. He hands LT. RYDER a notice.)

LIZ: Major Stephenson, sir, permission to speak.

MAJOR STEPHENSON: Not right now, ma'am. *(Motioning to LT. RYDER to give them their orders and exits.)*

(LT. RYDER hands the orders to LIZ.)

LIZ: Thank you, sir.

CATHERINE: What are they?

LIZ: We're to practice preflight check.

CATHERINE: Are they kidding?

MARY: That means we're getting closer to flying.

GERRY: I don't need to go hunting for bird nests in the guts of my propeller. Who the hell do they think we are?!

CATHERINE: Liz, I talked with Cochran; she did talk with the Major. I think it's time we talked with the Major. *(To LIZ.)* You know military protocol – *(LIZ glares at her.)*

LIZ: *(Not believing what she may be about to do.)* I'll talk to the Major.

(Snare drum riff. The WOMEN change formation. LT. RYDER does an about face and faces forward.)

LT. RYDER: Bridges, Sloane, Reade, and Nevelson! *(Pause.)* Bridges, Sloane, Reade, and Nevelson!

(MAJOR STEPHENSON enters.)

LT. RYDER: Sir, the men... well, the men...

MAJOR STEPHENSON: What the hell is goin' on here!

LT. RYDER: We've got a little problem here, sir.

LIZ: Major Stephenson, sir.

MAJOR STEPHENSON: Would you like to explain that to me?

LT. RYDER: Well, sir... *(Lowering his voice.)* We have a *FUBAR* here, sir. The men. The men. Sir.

MAJOR STEPHENSON: Yes, yes. What about the men?

LT. RYDER: They don't want to fly tow-target missions for the trainees, sir. They're even talking about...

LIZ: Major, permission to speak, sir.

MAJOR STEPHENSON: Hold on their, Mister... Miss. *(To LT. RYDER.)* Mister, start talkin'! We have artillery trainees looking up into the blue sky, and there's nothing comin' across. FUBAR or SNAFU - it is your ass, mister.

LIZ: Sir, I am requesting to speak with you now!

MAJOR STEPHENSON: You do not interrupt a superior officer!

LIZ: I am a civilian!

MAJOR STEPHENSON: Miss. I have got bigger problems!

LIZ: That we can solve, sir!

MAJOR STEPHENSON: You do not have a clue as to what my problem is!

LIZ: Your men are refusing to fly, sir! Is that not right, Ladies?

MARY: Affirmative!

GERRY: Affirmative!

CATHERINE: Affirmative!

MAJOR STEPHENSON: One hell of a minute. *(To LT. RYDER.) Hand me the roster, soldier. (LT. RYDER hands the roster to MAJOR STEPHENSON.)* Langley.

LIZ: Yes, sir.

MAJOR STEPHENSON: O'Connor.

MARY: Yes, sir.

MAJOR STEPHENSON: Watts.

CATHERINE: Sir.

MAJOR STEPHENSON: Hansen.

GERRY: Sir.

MAJOR STEPHENSON: Well, Miss Langley, you have my ears. *(Now that LIZ has his attention; she is speechless. She looks at the other women. They are giving her desperate looks. They want her to speak. She wants to speak. But she knows she has just stepped into a volatile situation. A situation that her father would tell her is "crossing the line.")* You know, that's funny. I'm not hearing anything. *(Silence.)* Cat got your tongue? Well, why don't I ask the questions? *(Silence and then he shouts this as if it were an order.)* Miss Langley, what the hell do you think you are doing interruptin' a superior officer?!

LIZ: *(In the following dialogue LIZ matches his volume and vocal pattern. She is ready for the challenge.*

LIZ (cont'd): (*IMPORTANT: During this scene, LIZ does not look at MAJOR STEPHENSON until the script specifies that she can. The protocol followed is of absolute importance to the stakes in this scene. LIZ is not comfortable in pursuing this; however, she has no alternative.*) I am interrupting for the sole purpose of solving your problem, sir. I am doing that, sir, by simply informing you of our orders, sir. Orders to fly tow targets, sir. We have been here for four weeks, sir. In that time, sir, while we have checked out on all specified planes, while we have spent hours in link training, classes, briefings, and test runs -- all of which we have passed with above averages, we have not been assigned one tow-target mission.

MAJOR STEPHENSON: You have that right, Langley.

LIZ: Well, sir.

MAJOR STEPHENSON: Langley, I have men who have just come from cadet training. They have priority. And they are giving me enough trouble. Their comment –

LIZ: I've heard it, sir.

MAJOR STEPHENSON: Have you?

LIZ: Yes, sir. In the ready room, sir.

MAJOR STEPHENSON: You have heard their comments in all their colorful language?

LIZ: Yes, sir. (*Repeating what she had heard and attempting to sound like a male cadet.*) I quote, sir: "If you think I am crazy enough to get my ass blown to bits flying tow-target training missions, you are a nutcase. If I'm gonna die it's going to be by some bastard Jap blasting me out of the sky -- not some 'wet-behind-the-ears-when-do-I-get-my-leave-so-I-can-go-fuck someone 'trainee'." End of quote, sir.

MARY: *(An intake of breath as she makes the sign of the cross.)* Ah!

GERRY: *(laughter unbecoming bursts out)* Holy cow!

(CATHERINE looks at LIZ. Surprise and pride are hard to hide. None of these WOMEN -- except, perhaps, CATHERINE have ever mouthed the word "fuck". Even LIZ is amazed when she repeats verbatim what she heard.)

MAJOR STEPHENSON: So. She's speaking for the three of you. *(The WOMEN nod.)* If you were my daughters, I'd wash your mouths out with soap.

LIZ: May I comment, sir?

MAJOR STEPHENSON: You know, for a civilian, you have this army talk down to a science.

LIZ: My Father's a master sergeant, sir.

MAJOR STEPHENSON: Well. *That* explains it.

LIZ: May I continue, sir.

MAJOR STEPHENSON: Only if you put yourself at ease. *(LIZ goes to "at ease" position. The other three WOMEN follow her lead.)* I didn't mean the rest of you. *(CATHERINE, MARY, and GERRY jump back into "attention" position.)* You ladies were never meant for this. At ease. *(To the other WOMEN.)* All of you. *(The WOMEN go to "at ease" position.)* Continue, Miss Langley.

LIZ: Yes, sir. Major, we know, sir, that the men who co-pilot on tow-target missions are reluctant to have women flying with them, and I know they have threatened to stand down.

STEPHENSON: Stand down?

LIZ: Yes, sir.

STEPHENSON: Go on.

LIZ: I know you have your hands full, and you are doing your utmost to soothe a very difficult situation. I respect that, sir.

MAJOR STEPHENSON: Flattery doesn't work, Langley. I'm sure your Father communicated that to you at a very early age. There's a war going on. And I'd like to get on with it.

LIZ: So would we, sir. What I am saying, sir, is that while I believe you have been doing your utmost to accommodate women flyers at Camp Davis; you have not done enough, sir.

MAJOR STEPHENSON: So you're dad taught you that you can say anything to a superior, just so long as you tack a "sir" at the end of it. Go on.

LIZ: Yes, sir. If your cadets are not eager to fly the tow-target missions, let us. One of two things will happen. We will do so poorly that we'll prove our superiors correct in saying "Women don't belong in the air."

MAJOR STEPHENSON: Or...

LIZ: Or we do so well that you see our worth, and the men can be released in greater numbers to fly combat.

MAJOR STEPHENSON: Or you do so well, that the men will want their jobs back.

LIZ: That is a possible result, sir.

MAJOR STEPHENSON: You got it.

LIZ: *(looking at MAJOR STEPHENSON)* Sir?

MAJOR STEPHENSON: Now, don't play sweet dumb thing with me. You got what you wanted. Report 0600. In fact, the whole damned lot of you are gonna report. Get your sleep tonight, girls. You'll need it.

LIZ: *(turns face front)* Yes, sir. Thank you, sir.

MARY: Yes, sir. Thank you, sir.

GERRY: Yes, sir. Thank you, sir.

MAJOR STEPHENSON: *(Looking at CATHERINE.)* No comment from you, Watts?

CATHERINE: Miss Langley represents me.

MAJOR STEPHENSON: Well, just so long as Miss Langley doesn't get too cocky. I have some not-so-classified information to give you and the other female pilots. Miss Cochran's champion, General Arnold, was on the line this morning ordering you to tow-targets. So don't think this one little meeting or Miss Cochran's hysterical calls to me changed my mind. And don't think Miss Cochran's going to be too pleased to know you talked directly to me about your problems. That's out of line. You should know that, Miss Langley. You're father taught you military protocol did he not? I could reverse this decision by simply telling General Arnold of this conversation, but I'm going to go that extra mile with you. You'll get your assignments. But never forget this. As far as I am concerned you are powder-puff pilots, and you do not belong here. The men in our forces die daily in the trenches, and my superiors have to take orders from a President who has never seen combat, politicians who make decisions that will get them re-elected, and high-pressured business-men who think that war is just another way to make money. But I am military.   (continued)

MAJOR STEPHENSON (Cont'd): I will follow my orders. But I want you to know that when you are on this base, there is an officer in charge of you that does not believe you belong here. I resent your presence. I don't give a damn if you turn out to be better than my men. You're still women. And in my book that means you are in the way. Now if there is nothing further to discuss –

LIZ: One more item, sir.

MAJOR STEPHENSON: Yes, Langley.

LIZ: Please inform your men that we are fellow flyers -- women, yes -- but fellow flyers. We are doing our job for the war. And if anyone of them asks "what we charge for our services" ever again, and I'm around to hear, I will personally box the living daylights out of him. He won't know what hit him. As a point of information, sir, I had four brothers, and they taught me to take care of myself. I don't know how to flirt, but I can beat the shit.. I mean...dickens... out of any man. Thank you, sir. *(LIZ, unable to comprehend that she has said "fuck" and "shit" to her superior officer, bolts to exit.)*

MAJOR STEPHENSON: Goddamn it, Langley, you are not dismissed! Attention! All of you! *(The WOMEN all snap to "attention".)* Now. As another point of information - I am not your spokesman. Dismissed! *(The WOMEN exit -- big smiles on their faces.)* God, I wish I had that bar of soap!

(Music explodes as the stage goes to black. After a three second count, the lights go into shadow. In the shadowed light WAYNE and the CONTROL TOWER OPERATOR place the four stools on stage and move to the upper level.

Each stool holds a flight jacket, a silk scarf and a clipboard. These stools represent the planes.)

LT. RYDER: *(In full voice.)* Take 'em up alone, Ladies.

(The light changes. The WOMEN run on cheering. Once they hit center you see them join their hands and like the musketeers of old shout.)

GERRY, LIZ, CATHERINE, MARY: One for all and all for one!

(In slow motion, the WOMEN approach their stools. The MEN in the flight sequence take their places on the platform steps above. JACQUELINE COCHRAN and MAJOR STEPHENSON are on opposite side of the stage under specials. WAYNE LANGHORN, LT. RYDER, and the ARTILLERY OFFICER are on the opposite side of the stage from JACQUELINE COCHRAN and MAJOR STEPHENSON: The four WOMEN are now facing upstage directly in front of their respective stool. Their backs are to the audience. The ritual donning of the bomber jacket, scarf and placement of the stool for flight is as follows: GERRY dons jacket; when GERRY has her jacket on and begins to place her scarf around her neck, MARY dons her jacket; then LIZ; then CATHERINE. Once each flier has donned the scarf, she picks up the clipboard and lifts the stool. Resting the stool on her hip, she slowly, in a fluid motion walks to her position, places the stool and sits. Once all the women are in position, the flight sequence begins. The orchestration of the music fades in and under the entire sequence. GERRY begins her speech as CATHERINE completes the ritual. As GERRY begins, the music fades under.)

GERRY: Check Form 1: We had engine and body parts that were older than Methuselah. But you checked -- propellers, rudders, tail wheels, tires -- before and after you flew. You marked in bright red if something was wrong. 'Course there was no guarantee that it could or would be fixed. But if you screwed-up -- on anything -- you'd get demerits. Seventy and you were out. The men could walk their demerits off. Not for us. For us, it was the ugly beginning to the inevitable end. So you checked your form, and you followed your checklist like it's the Bible.

(Music fades up and under this entire sequence until the end of the act. The women hold clip boards with pencils. Their particular flight check list is on their clipboard. The flight check is a celebration of sound and is also counterpoint to JACQUELINE COCHRAN'S and MAJOR STEPHENSON'S conversation with the unseen General. The conversation to the general begins when CATHERINE begins the phrase "priming engines". Once CATHERINE begins, the other WOMEN follow. This is a layering of words, sounds, and rhythms. The WOMEN overlap each other. The effect is fugue-like. CATHERINE, MARY, and LIZ are orchestrated so that GERRY's words begin to dominate, and at the end, GERRY's final lines end the beat.)

CATHERINE: Master switch on, generators on.

Check quadrant.

Throttles 3/4 of an inch open: mixture rich.

Carburetor air cold: propeller high pitch.

Tank selector to the fullest tank.

Engine selector to both; cross feed off.

Wobble pump, 4 strokes.

Priming engines -- cold -- six strokes.

Starting engines.

Push starter toggle switch.

Engine starting.

Apply carburetor heat to maintain 20 degree C.

Heat temperature -- minimum 100 degrees C, maximum 200 degrees Centigrade.

Maximum drop 1 ignition unit, 80 RPM.

MARY: Master switch on, generators.

Check quadrant.

Throttles 3/4 of an inch open: mixture rich.

Carburetor air cold: propeller high pitch.

Tank selector to the fullest tank.

Engine selector to both; cross feed off.

Wobble pump, 4 strokes

Priming engines -- cold -- six strokes

Starting engines.

Push starter toggle switch.

Engine starting.

Oil temperatures minimum 40 degrees C., maximum 100 degrees Centigrade.

Fuel pressure -- idling RMP 1/2 pound, cruising RPM 2 to 3 1/2 pounds.

LIZ: Check quadrant.
Throttles 3/4 of an inch open: mixture rich.
Carburetor air cold: propeller high pitch.
Tank selector to the fullest tank.
Engine selector to both; cross feed off.
Wobble pump, 4 strokes.
Priming engine -- cold -- six strokes.
Starting engines.
Battery ignition switch on.
Engine starting.
Warming up -- 800 to 1000 RPM
Oil pressure -- 60 to 90 pounds.
Engine moving to 1500 RPM -- propeller in low pitch.
Prepare for take-off -- check control.

GERRY: Master -- Switch -- Generators. Don't mess up.
Check - throttles - Check.
3/4 of an inch open -- propeller high pitch.
Carburetor -- propeller -- full tank.
Full tank -- engine selector -- cross feed off.
Cross feed off -- 4 stokes -- 4 strokes.
Priming engine -- priming engines.
Don't screw up, don't screw up!
Ignition switch on -- starting engines.
Engines starting -- Jeepers! I'm flying!
Let her go, baby! Let her go!
Oil pressure -- 60 to 90 pounds. That's it baby --
Warm-up for Gerry -- that's it baby!

(Separate specials on MAJOR STEPHENSON and JACQUELINE COCHRAN. They are both talking with the unseen General. This dialogue is under the preflight check of the WOMEN. Their dialogue takes focus as the preflight check dialogue supports MAJOR STEPHENSON and JACQUELINE COCHRAN.)

MAJOR STEPHENSON: General, it's bad enough that I am not over there fightin' combat, but putting me in charge of these girls - I've got two of my own, and they can't drive cars much less a plane. I'm not suggesting your wrong. Yes, sir!

JACQUELINE: *(Overlapping MAJOR STEPHENSON'S last sentence.)* Well, I am sorry that my girls talked with Major Stephenson, General. They were not followin' channels. I am most upset, and I will certainly let them know your extreme displeasure. I know they were protectin' me. Major Stephenson wasn't listening to me, and they are civilians. Lord, General, they're only trying to win the war -- isn't that what we're all trying to do. What are those little boys afraid of?

MAJOR STEPHENSON: General Arnold, I am not suggesting you are wrong, sir. I am saying that my men do not understand why these women are flying these missions. Yes, sir. Yes. That is true. My new cadets showed resistance. But if they see the women flying, don't you think we're sending a message that -- maybe they're right -- that the job isn't that important? Yes, General. Your orders are being followed. To the letter. Yes, sir -- they are doing pre-flight check as we speak.

(SOUND: As they do pre-flight check there is the sound of engines starting and the sound of the planes taking off. The women overlap their checklist ritual continuing to the

end of Major Stephenson's phone call with the general. If the checklist ends, the WOMEN repeat until the checklist builds and culminates with GERRY'S LINE.)

GERRY: We're moving -- Control tower, make way! This baby's flying -- this mama's moving out - Clear the runway -- it's mine all the way!

(MAJOR STEPHENSON and JACQUELINE COCHRAN are still talking with the unseen general. As GERRY shouts "clear the runway -- it's mine all the way", there is a visual of JACQUELINE COCHRAN hanging up the phone with a triumphant smile and MAJOR STEPHENSON hanging up the phone cursing all the way.)

ARTILLERY OFFICER: Well. We can all breathe a sigh of relief. The mission's accomplished.

LT. RYDER: If it's all the same to you. I wish the damn mission had been aborted.

ARTILLERY OFFICER: I don't like this anymore than you do, but the world's changing. Next thing you know, we'll be wearing the aprons.

LT. RYDER: When hell freezes over.

WAYNE: *(To LT. RYDER.)* Well, if that don't beat all. They look like real fliers to me, sir. Flyin' high... Flyin' straight...

LT. RYDER: *(Looking at WAYNE.)* Well, finish it, mister - smooth landing? Isn't that what you were going to say?

WAYNE: Yes, sir.

LT. RYDER: So say it, mister.

WAYNE: Sir, with these planes, smooth landin's are between you and your Maker.

(Sound of planes soar into the sky. The WOMEN mime in-flight flying. As sound of planes fades under, a light comes up on MARY.)

MARY: I can't tell you how tickled I am flying tow-target missions! When this war started, they wouldn't let women fly for the Civil Air Patrol 'cause they didn't want us flying near the coast. Now, we could fly up and down the coast and up to 50 miles out over the Atlantic. But here I was towing targets for artillery trainees. Me. The little Catholic kid from Minnesota. I remember dad said that out of all his children -- and there were fourteen of us -- how he never worried about me because I was the sensible one. Now, he keeps writing me letters saying that what I am doing is the most insane occupation any of his children have ever chosen. And now that I'm flying tow targets, I agree with him. Especially today. *(Under the music a separate SOUND OF ARTILLERY HITTING THE PLANE.)* That sound is machine gun bullets hitting my plane. And that's exactly what they did. They managed to miss the tow-target, which is actually this long, thirty-foot piece of muslin tied to the tail of my A-24. The tail of it mind you -- and their job is to figure out how fast the plane's going, so when they shoot their guns, the bullets travel at such a speed that they can hit their target when the plane reaches the designated area. And, I suppose, if you look at it that way -- they hit their target. That is -- if they were aimin' at the plane. Except as trainees they're suppose to aim at the tow-target, attached to my tail. The first time it happened, I started hic-cuppin' -- that's what I do when I get in a tight situation. I hiccup. (continued)

MARY (Cont'd): So there I was hic-cuppin' and while I was hic-cuppin' away, I politely radioed down and said *(MARY hic-cups.)* "Excuse me, I think one of your men is hitting me." *(End of hic-cups.)* A few seconds later the sounds of firing stopped, and then I heard on my radio - "Sorry, ma'am, one of our trainees thought he was suppose to hit the plane that had the white muslin streaming out behind it. We informed him of his error. It won't happen again. He would like to know if he could make this up by taking you out for a drink." I, of course, said *(Hic-cup.)* "thank you, but no -- because as we both knew, dating was against military rules, and besides, I didn't drink. When I got back to the base, I looked at my plane and sure enough there were six bullet holes in the fuselage -- that's about three inches from where my head had been. That night I had my first gin and tonic.

(The light on MARY fades out, as the music crescendos. There is a brief moment of the WOMEN in-flight, as the music fades under the light comes up on LIZ.)

LIZ: Flying to the training area for anti-aircraft artillery practice was no picnic, especially when you had some apprehensive serviceman ordered to target reel flying with you. There was one sweet kid -- no more than eighteen assigned to me, and he saw me coming, and I could hear in his mind –

SERVICEMAN: Holy Shit! It's a girl! What if the artillery men hit the plane instead of the tow-target?! What if she loses her cool? …What if she bails out and leaves me!? She's a civilian. She doesn't have to stay.

LIZ: Sure enough -- something happened -- oh, not so exciting as getting hit by real artillery fire -- no such luck. (continued)

LIZ (Cont'd): I had a bum plane, and just as we were headed down the beach to the gunnery positions, I smelled smoke -- and while I couldn't see the smoke –

SERVICEMAN: Ah, Langley -- ah, Miss Langley... there's a fire back here -- oh, please, Jesus, please, Jesus, don't be frightened, just keep calm.

LIZ: Think we can make it back?

SERVICEMAN: I think we can -- just stay calm. Maybe we should jump.

LIZ: I don't think so. Not at a thousand feet. *(Making radio contact.)* Tower Control, Tower Control -- there seems to be a little fire at my tail. Clear for emergency landing. And so the tower cleared for the emergency landing. By this time the smoke was building all around the cockpit. I could hear my man hitting the sides of his cockpit -- I don't know what he thought he was doing. But, he sure as hell was panicking. So I thought -- for his sake -- I was going to make this the smoothest landing I could -- besides, I had two gas tanks smack dab in the center section of the plane -- no sense blowing us apart. The landing was so smooth -- by the time the trucks got there, we had the fire under control. I never saw a more relieved young man in my life. I figured he needed a little comforting -- so after combing my hair, and reapplying my make-up, I got out of my cockpit and walked over to the young man. Smiling, I patted him on the shoulder, and said: good thing you were there -- it kept me calm. He smiled, hiked up his pants, filled with shit, and walked into the sunset.

(As the music crescendos, the spotlight fades out on LIZ and fades up on CATHERINE, as we hear her laughter.)

CATHERINE: God! Those tight-assed me-Tarzan, you - Jane pilots are starting to realize that there's more to us than Betty Crocker and Betty Grable. The same guys who wanted to quit because the "powder-puff" pilots were here, refused their transfers and wanted to hang around - to "help us, ladies". And why the change of mind? Because we flew harder than most any man on that base. And the pilots were willing to let us do it -- they had to uphold their motto -- "if we're gonna die, it'll be in combat not from some crazy-assed artillery trainee who doesn't know what he's supposed to shoot at!" So while they sat playing cards in the ready room, we graduated to A-25 dive bombers. Much more fun than tow-targets -- 'course in the ready-room the A-25 was known as the "coffin" -- called so because the planes were in such bad shape that it could very well end up being your resting place. But I've never cared much for safe flying -- so when Lt. Ryder was having a hard time getting the men assigned to fly the dive bombers and the gunnery officers were giving him flak, I said -- "I'll do it" –

LT. RYDER: Are you crazy, Lady? You've never done it before.

CATHERINE: That's right.

LT. RYDER: It's not tow-targets -- you're diving, and you have to pull that damn plane up when it's 200 feet from the ground -- it's no picnic. The plane crashes, you're charred meat.

CATHERINE: That's right.

LT. RYDER: I wouldn't feel right havin' you dive at gun positions.

CATHERINE: You just go ahead and not feel right. *(Pause.)* Sir.

LT. RYDER: We'll see about that. Miller! Bridges! You're on! *(Silence.)* Miller! Bridges!

CATHERINE: I believe I saw both of them headed for the dispensary -- after breakfast, of course. *(Silence)* Oh, come on, it looks like fun.

LT. RYDER: According to your records you have never done a dive bomb mission.

CATHERINE: Then I guess I should get started.

LT. RYDER: When they hear your voice, they'll abort the mission. They won't want a woman. Then I'll get the flak.

CATHERINE: *(Lowering her register.)* Did I ever tell you that when I'm on the phone, I'm sometimes mistaken for a man?

LT. RYDER: It's your funeral.

CATHERINE: Don't worry. I can afford it. *(Using lower register.)* Roger, reporting for assigned mission. This is my first time out -- just a rookie -- so tell me what you want. Roger and out.

ARTILLERY OFFICER: Roger. You're better than nothing. All right -- climb to 8,000 feet and start your dive to about 200 feet above the beach -- just pretend you want to bomb the bejesus out of us. Roger and out.

CATHERINE: *(To herself in her own voice.)* That's the best part of it. *(Low register.)* Roger -- it'll be my pleasure. Roger and out. *(In her own voice.)* And as I circled and started to climb -- 2,000 -- 3,000 -- 5,000 -- 7,000 -- and 8 -- Christ, I thought -- this is too good, this is too perfect -- this is -- start that dive – *(As CATHERINE starts her dive, the other WOMEN are following the identical flight pattern.)*   (continued)

CATHERINE (Cont'd): Goddamn, those men -- they've got it all -- and now so do I. Come on baby, let's push -- let's push -- so I began to dive 7,000 - 6,5,4,3 -- I was in a trance -- I was immortal. I was heading 1,000 feet -- and I saw the beach comin' at me. I pulled back on the stick and prepared for the 200 feet sweep up -- except the damn stick wouldn't pull back. The seven-ton coffin kept diving. If this is what death feels like, there's a lot to recommend it.

(The music fades out.)

ARTILLERY OFFICER: Good Lord, look at that flyer! How's he doin' that!

CATHERINE: I dug in and pulled at the stick -- the beach still coming at me -- I screamed -- pulled the stick even harder -- and blacked out. I came to a few seconds later -- and somebody up there was my copilot -- because I was level with the beach and climbin' up again!

ARTILLERY OFFICER: Officer, who is that cadet! He's first class!

LT. RYDER: One of the girls, sir.

ARTILLERY OFFICER: A female! Well, if that don't beat all! She went all the way! Simulated an actual attack! Scared the shit out of my men, and then did it twice more. Right on target, less than 200 feet! That's more assistance than they've gotten from the most seasoned pilots. They're going to keep that little lady busy.

CATHERINE: Yahoo! Geronimo! Coming in on approach!

(CATHERINE gets off her stool and places stool off the platform and moves to ready room area. Each woman, except for MARY, follows the same pattern until they are all back in the ready room. MARY remains on her stool as if she is taxing in.)

LIZ: Coming in on approach!

GERRY: Coming in on approach!

MARY: Coming in on approach!

GERRY: You really did that?!

LIZ: *(Simultaneous with CONTROL TOWER'S lines below.)* Holy Shit! They didn't know you blacked out?!

CONTROL TOWER: *(Simultaneous with LIZ'S line above.)* Taxi her in, Miss Mary – you are doin' mighty fine.

CATHERINE: *(Simultaneous with GERRY'S line below.)* Only way they would have known is if I had crashed.

GERRY: *(Simultaneous with CATHERINE'S line above.)* Would you look at our Miss Mary.

LIZ: *(Simultaneous with GERRY'S line below.)* How in the world –

GERRY: *(Simultaneous with LIZ'S line above.)* Oh, my God – there's a plane stalled.

CATHERINE: *(Simultaneous with CONTROL TOWER'S line below.)* Well, I'd like to say it was for God, Country – and –

CONTROL TOWER: *(Simultaneous with CATHERINE'S line above.)* Miss Mary, slow her down, slow her down.

GERRY: Would you guys shut up!

LIZ: My God!

CONTROL TOWER: There's a B-34 directly in front of you. Full brake, Miss Mary. Full brake. Full brake.

CATHERINE: What the hell is happening?!

LT. RYDER: She's gonna slam in -- slam in – slam in -- damn! damn! Who left that plane out there?

MARY: *(Simultaneous with CONTROL TOWER'S Lines below.)* Keep myself calm – calm – slow – brake – brake – slow brake – slow brake. Oh, dear Lord, I'm gonna hit.

CONTROL TOWER: *(Simultaneous with MARY's lines above.)* Coming too close. Coming too close.

LT. RYDER: Holy Moely, that plane just froze! She's tippin'! She's tippin'! Nose up!

(MARY executes a stylized braking of the plane and moves off the stool and places herself on the acting area opposite the ready room area. This should be a smooth transition. One scene leads to the other without changing the set pieces.)

GERRY: She didn't hit the plane. Thank God.

CATHERINE: God! I hope she's all right.

LIZ: She's fine! She's fine. She's a good flyer!

(MARY slides off the stool and goes to MAJOR STEPHENSON. LIZ, CATHERINE, and GERRY exit.)

MAJOR STEPHENSON: Who the hell do you think you're flying for? Hitler?

MARY: No, sir.

MAJOR STEPHENSON: That is a $60,000 plane! You damaged the propeller! And if you hadn't seen the other plane, Lord knows what condition both planes and you would have been in!

MARY: Sir, I was cleared for taxi, sir. All of a sudden I was heading right into the wing of a B-34. I jammed on my brakes -- my plane froze on the spot and over it went. The plane that was there had been left -- just left, sir. This is my first accident in over 750 hours of flying experience.

MAJOR STEPHENSON: *(Overlapping with Mary.)* 750 hours of flying experience! I know! I know! I have the report. Brakes readjusted -- not mentioned in the Form 1. That, my dear, is the only thing saving your ass. Do you understand me? Do you understand me?! I can't hear you. *(MARY starts hic-cupping uncontrollably.)* Stop it! *(MARY attempts to control her hic-cups, but she fails miserably.)*

MARY: Yes, sir. I'm trying, sir. It's just that when I -- *(Holds breath then a series of hic-cups comes out.)* -- I'm trying, Major.

MAJOR STEPHENSON: Just calm down. Calm down. *(He can't help but smile. MARY attempts to stop. She can't, and the hiccups get worse.)*

LT. RYDER: Should I get her some water, Lieutenant?

MAJOR STEPHENSON: Two glasses of water. *(LT. RYDER gets water. MAJOR STEPHENSON, absolutely helpless, watches her hiccupping.)*

MARY: *(Hiccupping throughout.)* I'm sorry, sir. I'm really sorry, sir.

MAJOR STEPHENSON: Hold your breath. I'll count to ten. Ready? *(MARY holds her breath and nods her head. As MAJOR STEPHENSON is counting, LT. RYDER comes in with the glass of water. He observes the following exchange.)* One. Two. Three. Four. Five. Six. Seven. Eight. Nine. Ten. *(MARY exhales and hiccups in a rapid succession.)*

LT. RYDER: *(Chuckling.)* Water - sir.

MAJOR STEPHENSON: Thank you, Lieutenant. *(MAJOR STEPHENSON hands the glass of water to MARY.)*

MARY: *(Hiccupping.)* Thank you, sir.

MAJOR STEPHENSON: Now swill it down. I mean just big ole' gulps. That's it. Good Girl. That should do it.

MARY: *(Hiccupping.)* Yes, sir.

(MARY starts to drink. MAJOR STEPHENSON watches intently, gently coaching. LT. RYDER can barely keep his composure.)

MAJOR STEPHENSON: That's it -- swill it down -- good tall glass of water. *(To LT. RYDER.)* Give me the other glass, soldier. *(MAJOR STEPHENSON takes one glass from MARY and gives her the other.)* Now, quick, drink this other one. *(MARY looks at him as if he's lost his mind. Then she hiccups.)* Do as I say! *(MARY gulps it down and at the end gives out an enormous belch that sends LT. RYDER into gales of laughter.)* Mister, you get the hell out of here. *(LT. RYDER exits laughing. MAJOR STEPHENSON looks at MARY who is mortified that she belched in front of a superior officer.)* You all right, now?

MARY: Yes, sir. I do apologize.

MAJOR STEPHENSON: You have some water dripping from your chin. Have a... my handkerchief.

MARY: That's all right, sir, I have one.

MAJOR STEPHENSON: Damn it! Take the handkerchief! That's an order!

MARY: Yes, sir.

MAJOR STEPHENSON: Sit down.

(MAJOR STEPHENSON has not realized there is no chair. However, LT. RYDER, within earshot, is there with a chair. LT. RYDER wears a smile filled with subtext. LT. RYDER places the chair and exits.)

MARY: Yes, sir. *(MARY sits. He stares at her for a moment.)*

MAJOR STEPHENSON: Can I get you a cup of coffee or something?

MARY: No, sir.

MAJOR STEPHENSON: 'Course not. You had your share of liquids. *(An uncomfortable silence.)* Mind if I have a cup of coffee?

MARY: No, sir.

MAJOR STEPHENSON: Lieutenant, mug of Java, pronto! *(Again, MAJOR STEPHENSON waits. He is staring at MARY. MARY is unaware of his fixed gaze. His look is one of total bafflement. He hasn't the slightest idea what to say or do. The idea of a woman assigned to him as a pilot is foreign. He can't "go by the book" because no book exists. The lieutenant enters with the coffee and exits.)* So. *(Pause.)* Where you from?

MARY: Minnesota, a little town, you wouldn't know it.

MAJOR STEPHENSON: Try me.

MARY: Oh. Well, a little place called Shotley.

MAJOR STEPHENSON: Near Red Lake.

MARY: Yes, sir.

MAJOR STEPHENSON: I've got a sister. Up and married a Yankee. They live in Big Falls.

MARY: Oh.

MAJOR STEPHENSON: Would you mind if I sit down?

MARY: No, sir.

MAJOR STEPHENSON: *(He sits)* Thank you. *(pause)* You miss home.

MARY: I miss my family.

MAJOR STEPHENSON: Of course.

MARY: Sir, I apologize, sir for the "spasmodic inhalation causing a closure of my glottis".

MAJOR STEPHENSON: Pardon me?

MARY: The "spasmodic inhalation causing a closure of my glottis" -- that's the dictionary term for a hic-cup, Major.

MAJOR STEPHENSON: *(Totally charmed.)* Oh.

MARY: I can't guarantee it won't happen again. It's what I do when I get in tight spots. My dad says it's better than crying or fainting dead away.

MAJOR STEPHENSON: I have more experience when a young women sheds a few tears than flys. I know how to deal with tears.   (continued)

MAJOR STEPHENSON (Cont'd): You take the young lady in your arms... *(Catches himself.)* ...or pat her on the head. *(Changing the subject.)* You got a real nice lake near Shotely. I've gone campin' there a lot.

MARY: Our family loves camping.

MAJOR STEPHENSON: So you like to camp?

MARY: Yes, sir. I love the outdoors.

MAJOR STEPHENSON: How did a nice corn fed girl like yourself get involved in this crazy war?

MARY: They let me fly.

MAJOR STEPHENSON: What I want to know is who had the crazy notion to let you learn to fly?

MARY: It's something I wanted to do.

MAJOR STEPHENSON: But how? Weren't you suppose to be learning to can preserves and bake and sew and tend to the family?

MARY: I can do all that, sir.

MAJOR STEPHENSON: Well, that's good. Very good.

MARY: But I also fly.

MAJOR STEPHENSON: How did you get interested?

MARY: Barnstorming. When I was six years old, daddy took me to a show. This flyer did somersaults in his plane. Dived, swooped up, down, around, over -- never missing a move -- he even had his partner walk the wing. I was dumbstruck -- it was better than a circus! It was better than the radio, the movies! It was better than church! To get that close to heaven. There wasn't anything so grand. And I said to my daddy -- when I grow up, I'm gonna fly one of those!   (continued)

MARY (Cont'd): He smiled and said -- save that for your baby brother! But, daddy, I don't have a baby brother. But, you will sweet pie -- you will. Well, I had eight brothers and five more sisters, and I was the only one who had the bad sense to want to fly.

MAJOR STEPHENSON: Well, Miss O'Connor, at least you know its bad sense.

MARY: I don't believe its bad sense. Mom and dad sure do. I guess its different sense. I'll be sure to launder your handkerchief and return it. I'd be a little embarrassed to give it to you now.

MAJOR STEPHENSON: Don't you have a young fella who wants you safe at home?

MARY: No, sir. I'm kinda shy.

MAJOR STEPHENSON: It's becoming.

MARY: Sir?

MAJOR STEPHENSON: Shyness. I mean, you don't expect it from a woman who would... well, want to be in a situation where there are a lot of men around.

MARY: Oh, I'm not here for the men, sir. I'm here to fly.

MAJOR STEPHENSON: And I'm here to win a war.

MARY: So am I, sir.

MAJOR STEPHENSON: But you don't have to be.

MARY: I guess that's the difference, sir. Most men are here because they have to be. We're here because we want to be.

(MARY walks away and is near the area where her plane crashed. WAYNE is there. The light fades out on MAJOR STEPHENSON.)

WAYNE: You all right, Miss Mary?

(MARY nods.)

WAYNE: Did Major Stephenson read you the riot act?

(MARY shakes her head.)

WAYNE: Don't feel like talkin'? I don't blame you. You'll be fine, ma'm. You're a good flyer. Don't let anyone tell you different.

(The WOMEN rush in as WAYNE exits.)

LIZ: Oh, Mary, that was something to see.

MARY: I am so sorry.

GERRY: Honey, the brakes hadn't been adjusted. You didn't know. It wasn't on the form 1. Right? *(MARY nods her head.)* If you'd have known that, you would have tested them before take off. Besides, when they clear you to taxi in, you don't expect to see another plane parked directly in your path. What the hell was it doing there anyway?

MARY: It has a blown tire; the pilot must have just left it there. He was probably angry because the tire blew. I mean all the tires are blowing. We need new tires. We ask for them, and they say the rubber has to go to the war effort.

GERRY: We're part of that war effort.

LIZ: The best equipment and supplies go to the front. We have to use what's left over. That's part of our job.

CATHERINE: So when our planes stall in midair because they've sent the high octane overseas; I'm suppose to thank them. Is that before or after I bail out of the plane?

LIZ: Nothing's happened.

GERRY: Yet.

(LT. RYDER enters.)

LT. RYDER: O'Connor. Congratulations. I see by the report you're still scheduled for night flying. That means you didn't wash out. Now remember, night flying is blind flying. You and your instruments. Do you think you can handle that?

LIZ: She can handle it just fine.

LT. RYDER: I'm sure she can. That was quite a little show you put on in the Major's office.

CATHERINE: Leave her alone, mister.

LT. RYDER: "Spasmodic inhalation with closure of the glottis" -- now that was what you call a real smart maneuver -- I bet you're real good at crying. All those womanly charms -- and you're ready to use all of them except for the ones we really need.

CATHERINE: It is time for you to wash out the latrine, soldier boy!

LT. RYDER: It's time for me to ask for a transfer. I joined up to fight a war, not sit around with fragile women! It was a plane you almost slammed lady. Nobody got killed. Hell, you weren't even injured. Except your pride. *(LT. RYER leaves.)*

GERRY: What the hell was he talkin' about? Spasmodic inhalation?

LIZ: What happened with the Major?

MARY: Well, you know, Liz, when I get nervous or excited, I hiccup. That's what he meant by spasmodic inhalation. He must have been listening in on my meetin' with the Major.

LIZ: Mary! You have got to learn to control that!

CATHERINE: What is so damned wrong with that?

MARY: It's not anything I can control, and he was a real gentleman about it -- I know it shouldn't have happened.

LIZ: Damned right.

MARY: You're right. Darn right.

GERRY/CAHERINE: Liz!

MARY: I just -- for a minute I –

LIZ: That goes in your report, damn it. That's something they can take and hold up and say -- you see, Miss Cochran, your girls can't handle anything -- They've got one hand on the throttle -- some crisis hits and they panic -- I can just hear that soldier now. Telling this story and then saying -- next thing you know, they'll be crying, fainting -- god knows what!

MARY: I'm sorry.

LIZ: You can't do that, Mary.

CATHERINE: Liz, some things we can't control.

LIZ: Well, she's got to control it!

MARY: I'm sorry. I really am. No one's ever –

LIZ: I don't want to hear excuses.

GERRY: Easy, Liz. It was only a hic-cup.

LIZ: Ladies, you don't understand. They have different standards for us. They don't want us, and if the Major wants to -- he could use this little incident to send us home.

GERRY: He's not going to use this. Hell, we're doing jobs the guys don't want to touch. They're even telling us now when the missions are coming, so we can volunteer before their assigned. The Major knows a good thing. You're blowing this way out of proportion.

MARY: No, she's not.

CATHERINE: Oh, come on. There's nothing wrong with *(Laughs.)* hiccups. It's funny. I bet the Major thought it was funny to.

MARY: He was very polite. *(Beat.)* I don't mean the hiccups. *(To all the women.)* There's something wrong with us.

LIZ: What do you mean?

MARY: We've changed. We're afraid to smile or joke because it might be taken the wrong way. We try to outdo every male pilot. Fly higher, closer, faster. It's just not normal.

CATHERINE: War is not normal. We're in a war.

MARY: I know. But when he talked to me, and I looked into his eyes -- he has the most beautiful eyes. They're gentle. Did you know that?

LIZ: I hadn't noticed.

MARY: Well, they are. And I believe that he believes that in fighting against us, he's protecting us.

CATHERINE: I think she has a crush on our Major.

MARY: I just said he had beautiful eyes.

LIZ: There's no time for that.

GERRY: Liz, come on, we all have feelings.

LIZ: There's a war on damn it. Your feelings don't count! Jesus! I stuck my neck out for you. I did the talking for all of us. Now you listen to me, and you listen good. This is what we do. You double check every damn part of the plane, whether it is on Form 1 or not, and just like the men, refuse to fly if anything -- no matter how insignificant -- if it is red-marked.

MARY: But I always check.

LIZ: Yes, but this time you double check. In fact, you find out who the last mechanic that worked on the plane was, and go talk to him.

MARY: What if he's off duty?

LIZ: Then insist on another plane.

CATHERINE: Well, that's a fine way to win friends and influence people.

LT. RYDER: *(Off-stage.)* O'Connor report to the ready desk on the double.

MARY: *(Hears LT. RYDER'S voice and has an intake of breath and bears down hard and hiccups.)* Ah!

CATHERINE: What's wrong, Hon?

MARY: I don't know. Funny, I heard his voice say report and... *(Takes a deep breath.)* -- I'm fine.

LIZ: Don't you dare go into a fit.

CATHERINE: That's enough, Liz.

GERRY: Mary, I'm not called until tomorrow. We can trade off if you want.

MARY: Maybe that would be a good idea.

LIZ: It's a lousy idea. That's all they have to hear is Mary is not flying tonight. They'll say the women are chickening out.

CATHERINE: Well, let's just say she got her "friend". They don't want us to fly with our friend. Remember, it makes us hysterical.

MARY: That would be lying.

LIZ: Mary, you will do fine.

GERRY: Liz, I can trade with her.

LIZ: No.

CATHERINE: Liz!

LIZ: No. Mary. Remember what Miss Cochran said to us? Don't give the men any ammunition to stop this program. It's all on our shoulders.

LT. RYDER: *(Off-stage)* O'Connor, I repeat. Report to the operations desk immediately.

LIZ: Now you can do it. It wasn't even an accident. Come on, where's that barnstormer personality. You're not going to let an old B-34 with a lousy flat-tire stop you from helping the war effort? You're not going to let some smarmy, sleazy, slimy soldier boy scare you off? We have as much right to do our job and even make mistakes as the next fella. Don't let them take that right away from you.

GERRY: She can have that right tomorrow night when she's calmer.

MARY: I can do it.

LIZ: That's my Mary.

GERRY: You take it easy. And when you get nervous -- hiccup all you want -- hell, belch if you want. They should be thankful you don't pass gas. *(MARY exits. GERRY laughs at her own joke and turns to see CATHERINE staring LIZ down.)*

CATHERINE: Don't you have a sympathetic bone in that body of yours?

LIZ: Pardon me?

CATHERINE: You have crossed the line. Who the hell do you think you are?!

LIZ: I know exactly who I am. My purpose is very clear. And Damnit, my goals are noble.

CATHERINE: Purpose? Noble? Jesus, Liz. Who taught you to talk that way?

LIZ: And I don't want anyone or anything messing it up!

CATHERINE: She shouldn't be flying.

LIZ: No one forced her.

CATHERINE: Like hell!

GERRY: You girls shouldn't be fightin'.

CATHERINE: We're not all flying for revenge.

LIZ: That's enough.

CATHERINE: But you're flying for revenge. Aren't you? Those Japs killed your brother and every time you take a plane up, way in the back of your mind you are hoping that one of those infantry recruits blasting away at your tow-targets will shoot down the bastard that killed your brother. You don't care about freeing the world from fascists. This is personal.

LIZ: That is a lie!

CATHERINE: Like hell it is.

LT. RYDER: *(Off-stage.)* Langley and Watts -- report immediately.

GERRY: Well, since nobody wants me to fly tonight, I'll go do my laundry.

LIZ: *(To CATHERINE.)* Are you coming or aren't you?

(CATHERINE doesn't answer.)

GERRY: I meant it when I said you're blowing' this way out of proportion. Now come on, the G.D.O. Jughead was right. And I hate admittin' that. It was just a plane she hit. She didn't get hurt. And even though I think she should call it a night and have a few drinks at the club, she's flying. We're all flyin'. Isn't that why we're here? Now are you ladies going to call a truce? Remember? One for All? Come on, Catherine, you like night flyin'. It's dangerous. Almost as good as sex.

CATHERINE: Almost.

GERRY: Now, come on, kiss and make-up. We've got a war to fight. Well, you do. I'm doin' my laundry. *(GERRY exits.)*

LIZ: You coming?

CATHERINE: Don't you ever yell at Mary like that again. And over a hiccup! My God, Liz. You need to start drinking!

LIZ: Talk to me when the war is over!

(As CATHERINE and LIZ move to the downstage area. MARY walks in slow motion to the highest level on upstage center -- as she is positioning herself, WAYNE comes to where CATHERINE and GERRY wait.)

WAYNE: *(Talking to an unseen mechanic in training.)* Damn it, misters! If I find one more rag in a gas tank! If I find another drop of water in the goddamn carburetors, I'm putting you on report! Do you hear me! *(To LIZ AND CATHERINE.)* I'll be with you in a minute, ladies!

(The lights fade up on another acting area. The light reveals the ARTILLERY OFFICER and the ARTILLERY TRAINEE preparing to fire at the tow-target attached to MARY'S plane.)

ARTILLERY OFFICER: *(Speaking into the radio.)* Ready when you are, Sugar Charley. *(To ARTILLERY TRAINEE.)* How are you doin' soldier?

ARTILLERY TRAINEE: Just great! We got a bet going. Cigarettes. The greens are gonna beat the shit out of the blues!

ARTILLERY OFFICER: Just keep it steady. Control, mister. Control. Pure and simple.

ARTILLERY TRAINEE: You got it, sir.

CATHERINE: *(To WAYNE.)* We're headin' out.'

WAYNE: I'm afraid not. Your planes are disabled.

ARTILLERY OFFICER: Give it more lead! Give it more lead!

ARTILLERY TRAINEE: Yes, sir!

LIZ: What?

WAYNE: I got a call into control tower to pull Miss O'Connor's plane back in! She had the wrong report. Her plane is red-marked – She's circling now.

ARTILLERY TRAINEE: Here goes, baby face -- moving up, moving out and – *(The sound of artillery fire repeats over the following dialogue.)*

ARTILLERY OFFICER: More lead, soldier.

ARTILLERY TRAINEE: *(Singing – the tune "Yes, Sir, That's My Baby.)* Yes, sir, hit my baby -- no sir, I'm not navy. Yes, sir, shoot that baby down!

ARETILLERY OFFICER: Take it easy, soldier. Take it easy, soldier. Okay, comin' up – Give it more lead!

ARTILLERY TRAINEE: Come on, Lieutenant -- I need those cigarettes.

ARETILLERY OFFICER: Give it more lead, soldier.

MARY: Sugar Charley, we are headin' out.

CONTROL TOWER: Return to base now, Miss O'Connor. We had a wrong reading on your plane. It's got some problems. Just bring her back in.

MARY: Yes, sir. We're pullin' in the sleeve now.

CONTROL TOWER: See you back here.

ARETILLERY OFFICER: It's comin' now -- take it slow –

ARTILLERY TRAINEE: I do love live ammunition! And -- *(He mimics the sound of rapid fire.)*

ARTILLERY OFFICER: Holy Shit! *(He attempts to snatch the gunner's hand from the trigger.)*

(A split second after the ARTILLERY TRAINEE mimics the sound, the actual rapid fire resonates as it hits the plane.)

MARY: Oh, dang it, they hit my plane again. Excuse me, fellas, you're firin' -- *(Rapid fire and another hit.)* Holy Cow! Sugar Charley! They're aimin' at the dang plane again, and it's scarin' me spitless. *(She begins to hiccup.)*

ARTILLERY OFFICER: Jesus Christ! Mister! That was the plane!

ARTILLERY TRAINEE: Oh, Jesus!

ARTILLERY OFFICER: You all right up there!?

MARY: *(Trying to bring her hiccups under control.)* It's a hit. I'm headin' back, Sir. Lt. Robillard is with me. We've got it under control.

ARTILLERY OFFICER: I repeat. Are you all right?

MARY: Except for a few hiccups, I'm great, sir. *(Hiccups.)*

ARTILLERY OFFICER: Hiccups, hell. If I were up there, I'd be shittin' in my pants. You just get back safe, ma'am.

ARTILLERY TRAINEE: Oh, Jesus, did I just hit a female! Oh, Christ! Oh, Christ!

ARTILLERY OFFICER: That's enough, mister! Keep your trap shut! *(To Control Tower Operator.)* Who was flyin' that plane, Mister?

TOWER CONTROL: Miss O'Connor, sir.

ARTILLERY OFFICER: Oh, Jesus.

MARY: *(Hiccup.)* Sugar Charley. Sugar Charley. Seems like the plane's stalling -- I'm preparing for an emergency landing.

CATHERINE: Something's wrong. She's having trouble!

LIZ: God! Let's get to the runway! *(CATHERINE and LIZ run off.)*

WAYNE: Ladies! No! Don't go out there! No! Jesus! The Major's gonna have my ass! *(WAYNE runs after them.)*

TOWER CONTROL: Miss O'Connor, better bail out -- if the plane is stalling -- the instruments will read faulty -- even if we put the runway lights on, you won't be able to see the trees -- ready for bale out -- we'll meet you down there for dinner.

MARY: The Lieutenant and I are bailing out. Well, this certainly scared the hiccups out of me.

TOWER CONTROL: Just bail out, ma'am.

MARY: I can't. The latch is broken. It's broken. Oh, God –

(CATHERINE and LIZ run on from the other side of the stage. They are looking directly out over the audience, as if seeing the plane coming down for the landing. They are followed by WAYNE.)

TOWER CONTROL: Christ -- we're on our way -- try to get over those trees -- try –

MARY: I can't -- I can't -- I'm coming down.

WAYNE: Please, ladies, you can't be out here.

CATHERINE: Jesus Christ! She's out of control! The plane split. She's hittin' the trees!

LIZ: Oh, my God! Oh, my God! Mary! Mary!

WAYNE: Oh, no! Oh, no!

TOWER CONTROL: Oh, Christ -- I see her -- she's heading' for the swamp! Jesus! She's not going to make it!

MARY: Hail, Mary, full of grace, the Lord is with these. Blessed art thou among women, and blessed is the fruit of thy womb, Jesus. St. Anthony, help me out here! St. Christopher -- oh, please, Jesus, get me down safe, get me down safe -- Oh, Jesus, Jesus, Jesus, Jesus, Jesus, Jesus, Jesus. *(Screams)* Jesus!

(Blackout. END OF ACT ONE.)

Act Two

(Piano arrangement of "Balm in Gilead" – the selection should be reflective and meditative. It plays throughout the next scene. Lights up on LIZ center stage. Stage left area lights up on the ARTILLERY OFFICER, and ARTILLERY TRAINEE. Stage right area lights up MAJOR STEPENSON and THE LIEUTENANT.)

LIZ: I forced myself to remember the words of my Father. If you are to serve, you cannot care, you cannot love, you cannot want.

ARTILLERY TRAINEE: Permission to speak to her parents. To say I'm so sorry.

ARTILLERY OFFICER: Permission denied.

MAJOR STEPHENSON: Lieutenant, at ease.

PILOT: She could have survived, sir. Gettin' hit by a trigger happy trainee happens. It's nothin' new.

MAJOR STEPHENSON: Lieutenant –

LIZ: When I heard the plane crash, when I heard her screaming, flames soaring – I cared, I loved, I wanted her to live.

ARTILLERY TRAINEE: I killed a civilian.

ARETILLERY OFFICER: It was an accident. *(Silence.)*

PILOT: She could have survived if that damn cockpit latch had worked.

LIZ: I wanted my brother back. I wanted this war over. I wanted Donald holding me. I wanted someone to say this job is too tough. Go home.

ARTILLERY TRAINEE: I killed a female. *(Silence.)*

ARETILLERY OFFICER: We need to make our report.

LIZ: But none of that happened.

PILOT: I saw form one – the latch, but it was considered a minor problem, Sir. I should have said, no. No. We're not flyin'. I could have said that.

LIZ: And her screaming didn't stop.

MAJOR STEPHENSON: Just make your report.

ARTILLERY TRAINEE: And then?

ARETILLERY OFFICER: We go on to our next assignment.

PILOT: I don't remember much after... the plane shuddered – then I don't remember – I don't.

MAJOR STEPHENSON: Well, you made it down alive, Lieutenant.

LIZ: All the running, all the distance, all the time, none of it would ever silence her.

ARTILLERY TRAINEE: Sir?

ARETILLERY OFFICER: I can't answer your questions, soldier. I can't even answer mine.

LIZ: There was no choice but to stay. It wasn't enough, but it's the only thing that began to make sense.

(Lights out on LIZ: Lights up in the CATHERINE and GERRY area. The same lighting as the top of Act One. They wear their dresses from Act One.)

CATHERINE: Liz cried that night. Did you know that? *(GERRY shakes her head.)* She hid in the supply closet. I couldn't sleep. I saw her bed empty -- walked down the hall and heard her. I knew she was hiding from us. She'd rather die than let us see her cry. She was weeping like a baby. I wanted to open that closet and hold her. But part of me was so angry. If she hadn't pushed Mary into flying...

GERRY: Then I would have been dead. (An embarrassed silence.)

CATHERINE: I looked for you after the accident. Where did you go?

GERRY: I didn't run away if that's what you're thinking. They ordered us away. So I left. I -- silly -- I'd been doin' my laundry. I heard screams coming from the barracks. I saw you all haulin' ass across the field. I followed. When I saw what had happened, I couldn't go back with you. I just couldn't. I'd left my clothes in the washhouse. So I headed back there. This dress was hanging. It was dry -- I ironed it. Then I put it on. I wanted to be somewhere else. Anywhere but here. The dress made me feel –

CATHERINE: ... like a woman?

GERRY: Free. *(Pointedly.)* I've never had a problem feelin' like a woman. *(As GERRY continues to speak, she walks into another lighted area. LT. RYDER is there in subtle shadow. Lights out on CATHERINE. CATHERINE exits in the black.)* When I saw Mary's plane go down -- knowin' it could have been me -- it was as if my mind split in two. I needed to remember who I was. Not some uniform -- not that anyone cared a hoot what that uniform stood for -- particularly when we were wearin' it. The dress helped. (continued)

GERRY (Cont'd): A little. I stood outside -- there was a breeze. You know that feelin' when there's this whisper of a breeze that sneaks under the dress and caresses your body. I let myself sit down in the feelin'. It gave me a sense of comfort.

LT. RYDER: *(He is carrying a bottle of whiskey.)* Care for a nip?

GERRY: Where did you get that?

LT. RYDER: Actually. From your side of the farm. You ladies hide this underneath your barracks -- sort of like a little garden.

GERRY: None of your own?

LT. RYDER: I was comin' from the airstrip. Your supply is closer. Sure you don't want some?

GERRY: No thank you.

LT. RYDER: Sure is nice to see you in a dress. *(Silence.)* Lady, the last thing on my mind is what you think is on my mind. *(GERRY smiles sadly. LT. RYDER offers her the bottle.)* Can this G.D.O. offer you some of your own whiskey?

GERRY: Sure. *(Takes a swig.)* Thank you.

LT. RYDER: Anytime. Mind if I sit down?

GERRY: No.

LT. RYDER: I'll sit over here so you don't think I'm being fresh. *(Silence.)*

GERRY: How did she look?

LT. RYDER: You don't want to know, ma'am.

GERRY: I do.

LT. RYDER: Like a dead person looks. Ever seen a dead person?

GERRY: No.

LT. RYDER: Me neither. Lost my cherry on that one. That's why *(He indicates the bottle.)* ...that's why I can look at you, dressed like that, and shit, you're gorgeous, but not tonight, not now. *(GERRY reaches for the bottle. He passes it to her.)* I thought I was gonna see all kinds of death. Combat, you know. My first dead body is a female that shouldn't have been here in the first place. Goddamn you!

GERRY: We wanted to be there. They ordered us away.

LT. RYDER: They should have let you stay. They should have let you see what it's like to lift someone out of the ashes -- torn, bleeding -- I was pickin' her up in pieces.

GERRY: No.

LT. RYDER: You should've carried her away. Maybe that'd make it real for you.

GERRY: *(After a pause with difficulty and, yet, certainty.)* I would appreciate if you would place your arms around me and hold me. *(Silence.)* I know my own mind.

LT. RYDER: And tomorrow?

GERRY: *(She looks at him.)* It's as if nothin' ever happened.

(GERRY and LT. RYDER stare at each other. GERRY walks towards LT. RYER as the lights fade out on the two of them and up on CATHERINE and LIZ. CATHERINE is dressed once again in her flight suit.)

CATHERINE: Can't sleep. *(Silence.)* I heard you. *(Silence.)*

LIZ: Just sniffles. Summer sniffles.

CATHERINE: Sure.

LIZ: You hate me? *(CATHERINE shakes her head.)* I called Don.

DONALD: *(Shaking himself from sleep.)* Honey?

LIZ: I know it's late.

DONALD: No... it's fine. Has something happened?

LIZ: I just wanted to hear your voice.

DONALD: Something's happened.

LIZ: I miss Jason. Don't you?

DONALD: He was my best buddy.

LIZ: I miss him a lot. Do you think he died quickly?

DONALD: His ship was destroyed, sweetheart. Honey –

LIZ: Do you think he's in heaven?

DONALD: Elizabeth has someone died?

LIZ: I believe he is.

DONALD: Liz, you don't sound good.

LIZ: I just miss you.

DONALD: Can you get a three-day pass? I'll drive down. Norfolk isn't too far from where you are.

LIZ: We could get married.

DONALD: *(Pause.)* Liz, I thought you wanted to wait until the war was over.

LIZ: It was a silly idea. A three-day pass -- we could –

DONALD: What about your folks? My folks?

LIZ: They'll understand.

DONALD: I don't know if I do.

LIZ: It's either yes or no.

DONALD: Of course, it's yes. It's just that you were so –

LIZ: I know what I said; I changed my mind.

DONALD: I can get a pass in two weeks.

LIZ: I'll see you in two weeks.

DONALD: Lizzie.

LIZ: Yes.

DONALD: When this war is over, we can still have that big wedding -- I sure would like to see you all dolled up with a bouquet of buttercups and marigolds.

LIZ: I'd like that.

DONALD: I love you, baby.

LIZ: I love you too. *(Back to CATHERINE.)* You think I'm squirrley.

CATHERINE: No. I don't think you're squirrley. *(Silence.)*

LIZ: *(Looking up at the stars)* I bet Mary's one of those stars.

CATHERINE: What?

LIZ: Jason used to say that when someone died a new star was born. On his tombstone we put a star. Jason is a star. Now Mary.

CATHERINE: Well, let's hope we don't have any more stars for awhile. *(WAYNE enters.)*

WAYNE: Shouldn't be out here, ladies.

CATHERINE: Is that an order?

WAYNE: Oh, no, ma'am. I'm just a civilian like yourself. I just meant you might catch a chill. These cool southern nights are deceivin'.

CATHERINE: We're fine.

WAYNE: I'm sorry about Miss O'Connor.

CATHERINE: It was a stalled plane. There was nothing you could do.

WAYNE: Nothing. *(Silence.)*

LIZ: It was a stalled plane?

WAYNE: Maybe. There are only about three planes fit to fly. Her plane hadn't had an overhaul in over 500 hours. That's about 200 tow-target missions and God knows what else. Not an overhaul in sight. Hell, if it's not lousy planes' it's trigger-happy trainees. No wonder the men don't want to fly.

CATHERINE: What are you telling us?

WAYNE: Nothin', ma'am.

(As WAYNE leaves, the women look at each other. CATHERINE gets up and leaves in the opposite direction.)

LIZ: Where are you going?

CATHERINE: Miss Cochran's been on base for the last two hours.

(Lights down on LIZ, as CATHERINE walks into lighted acting area where JACQUELINE stands.)

JACQUELINE: Maybe? Langhorn said maybe?

CATHERINE: Yes. It wasn't just a stalled plane.

JACQUELINE: He shoulda' been horsewhipped for saying anything to my girls.

CATHERINE: Something else happened.

JACQUELINE: I've been here since 0200, Miss Watts. I know what has been said and hasn't been said. I am looking out for all of you. And I am depending on all my women – especially you.

CATHERINE: Then tell me what happened.

JACQUELINE: It's on a need to know basis. I'm protecting you. I'm protecting all of you.

CATHERINE: And Mary –

JACQUELINE: We'll talk about it later.

CATHERINE: We'll talk about it now.

JACQUELINE: Catherine, I don't like this anymore than you do, but don't think I'm an elite member of some sort of inner circle that protects me against what the real feelings are towards women flying. I'm not dealing with just an accident – an accident, by the way, that can happen to a man or a woman. I'm dealing with a legacy – a legacy that will place women where they belong –˙side by side with men, equal with men. Don't you want that as well? Don't let your personal matters get in the way of national concerns.

CATHERINE: I don't know if I can do that.

JACQUELINE: Then you be gracious enough to stand by me in silence.

LT. RYDER: *(Off stage.)* Ladies, ready room on the double.

(Lights up full as LT. RYDER, MAJOR STEPHENSON, LIZ, and GERRY are waiting.)

MAJOR STEPHENSON: Miss Cochran.

JACQUELINE: Thank you, Major. *(Taking her place with the other Officers.)* I know the death of one of our own brings the tragedy of this war close to us all. And I am sure that Miss O'Connor's family is grateful for your generous contribution to her funeral services. They are not a wealthy family, and they were touched by your concern.

GERRY: Will there be an investigation?

CATHERINE: *(Whispering.)* Not now, Gerry.

GERRY: *(Whispering.)* I could have been on that damned plane. I have a right to know.

JACQUELINE: I didn't hear that question.

GERRY: I said. Are you having a full out investigation?

JACQUELINE: The proper report is in the process of being drawn. There is no need for an investigation.

GERRY: Maybe someone is covering up what really happened.

LIZ: *(Under her breath.)* Gerry!

CATHERINE: *(Whispering.)* Easy, Gerry -- I've talked with Cochran.

GERRY: I don't care if you talked to God Almighty.

MAJOR STEPHENSON: *(To JACEQUELINE.)* I will respond. *(To GERRY.)* You have a lively imagination, Miss Hansen. There is no cover-up. Whatever happened on final approach was pilot error. Unfortunately, the latch on the canopy did not function so she could not escape.

GERRY: The nonfunctional canopy was the luck of the draw. Is that what you're saying, Major Stephenson? Sir?

(MAJOR STEPHENSON looks at JACQUELINE COCHRAN. It is obvious he is not pleased with the way her women are responding.)

MAJOR STEPHENSON: *(To the WOMEN.)* It was a great misfortune. We all cared for Miss O'Connor. She was a good flyer. Even good flyers make mistakes.

GERRY: There were no mistakes, Major.

JACQUELINE: You have misspoke, Miss Hansen. And you will cease speaking immediately. Now. A full report will be issued within the week. The memorial service will take place at 1500 in the chapel. We look forward to your attendance.

LIZ: Is her family here, Miss Cochran?

JACQUELINE: The family is not allowed on the base. You are dismissed. *(MAJOR STEPHENSON stops to speak with JACQUELINE. She turns to the WOMEN.)* Ladies do not leave yet.

MAJOR STEPHENSON: A message from General Arnold, Miss Cochran.

JACQUELINE: Yes?

MAJOR STEPHENSON: Keep your women under control.

(MAJOR STEPHENSON exits. LT. RYDER begins to follow MAJOR STEPHENSON but notices the WOMEN quietly arguing and stops. JACQUELINE moves to the WOMEN.)

JACQUELINE: Just what the hell do you think you were doing out there, missy?!

GERRY: This whole thing stinks of cover-up.

JACQUELINE: You've been reading too many "Black Mask" magazine stories. Now, Ladies, we are all on schedules; we all have planes to fly, and you are wasting precious time.

GERRY: Well, with our planes, Miss Cochran, our schedules could be aborted at any moment.

JACQUELINE: You are trying my good nature, Miss Henson.

LIZ: We apologize for Miss Henson, Miss Cochran, it's just –

JACQUELINE: I know. I know. This is a difficult time for all of you. I want to help, but there are channels.

CATHERINE: I think we just want to be assured that there will be an investigation, and I know that is exactly what you will do.

JACQUELINE: It's not appropriate to the situation.

CATHERINE: *(Stunned.)* What?

JACQUELINE: You heard me.

GERRY: What's not appropriate, Miss Cochran? Someone's been putting water in the damned carburetors. There have been rags left in gas tanks. God knows –

JACQUELINE: Rags in tanks, water in the carburetors. Hell, I know a pilot once found a vacuum cleaner in the tank -- the mechanic was cleaning it out, the lunch whistle blew and off he went leaving the vacuum cleaner in the damn tank. It was careless; it was dangerous, but it is not a reason to call for an investigation. There are some matters that are better left unsaid.

CATHERINE: Why for God's sakes?

JACQUELINE: *(JACQUELINE notices LT. RYDER.)* Did you want something, Lieutenant?

LT. RYDER: No, ma'am. I simply wished to convey my sincere sympathy to these young ladies.

JACQUELINE: Oh behalf of them I thank you. And now if you'll excuse us.

LT. RYDER: Certainly, ma'am. Ladies.

CATHERINE: Just a minute, Lieutenant.

JACQUELINE: I have dismissed him, Miss Watts.

CATHERINE: I understand the serviceman who was flying with her survived.

LT. RYDER: Yes. ma'am. He did not have the faulty canopy.

CATHERINE: Can we speak with him?

(LT. RYDER looks to JACQUELINE.)

JACQUELINE: You have been dismissed, Officer.

LT. RYDER: *(Making his own decision.)* He's been transferred ma'am.

GERRY: Transferred? Why the hell –

JACQUELINE: Thank you, Lieutenant... You are dismissed -- *(To CATHERINE.)* Miss Watts, you see that man. He's waiting for us to crack. He's achin' for us to throw in the towel. Now are you on my side or are you not?

CATHERINE: Jackie...

JACQUELINE: Miss Cochran.

CATHERINE: Miss Cochran. We just want some questions answered.

JACQUELINE: Do not expect answers. Simply follow your damn orders.

GERRY: Until we get some answers we won't be following orders.

LIZ: Please, ladies!

JACQUELINE: All right. Here's your answer. These men do not want women flying. If we place any attention on us except how great we are, they'll scrap us - without a thought. Do you want that to happen? *(Silence.)* Do you think I like dealing with some of these men -- I am fighting for you as best I can within the situation. Now, you want to make an issue of Mary dying and shut this program down? Is that what Mary would have wanted?

GERRY: So you're saying we have to just keep going.

JACQUELINE: I am saying that these gentlemen don't ask for us much, and when they do, you've got to do it. You've got to out think them, out do them, out show them. 'Cause if you don't, they'll say they were right. We don't have the fortitude, the guts. So you have to do it -- you have to.

GERRY: You really flew all those planes.

JACQUELINE: Damned right, I did. And I'd fly them again. I'd just make damn sure everything is in the best working order as possible.

GERRY: As possible. You mean make sure you can get out once you're in.

JACQUELINE: Get it into your head, Miss Hansen -- there is a war on. We are not the priority. If you wanted priority -- if you wanted Loretta Young making a movie about you -- then you should have joined Nancy Love's fliers -- they're the glamour queens -- the flygirls.

CATHERINE: That was unnecessary, Miss Cochran.

JACQUELINE: Yes, it was unnecessary, and I sincerely regret -- *(GERRY turns to leave.)* Damn you, Miss Hansen. Don't you leave until you have been dismissed. You are tryin' my patience.

GERRY: We just want the truth ma'am.

JACQUELINE: Well, you've got it. And I'll start with a story. A true story. You like stories don't you. *(Not waiting for an answer.)* -- I want you to chew on this story real hard. One of Mrs. Love's pilots was flying with a group of men and one of the gentlemen decided to play chicken with her. She didn't know what the hell was going on -- he was buzzing the hell out of her -- she tried to dive away, their wings met, and she went down. He made it to final approach. She didn't. While it was his fault -- his crime he wasn't even court martialed and why? Because he is a man, and they needed him for combat. Now, if Mrs. Love's WAFS can go on after experiencing that little episode -- so can we.

LIZ: Jesus!

GERRY: Do you believe it was pilot error?

JACQUELINE: Doesn't matter a bat's ass what I believe.

CATHERINE: Can we see the plane?

JACQUELINE: It broke in half. There is nothing but pieces. Besides, you were so hysterical when her plane crashed Major Stephenson ordered the site off limits to you ladies. I don't want to give him any more reasons to complain to General Arnold.

LIZ: You didn't hear her screams.

JACQUELINE: I have told you the truth as I see it. *(silence)* If there's no further questions, I have –

GERRY: ... a plane to fly. Miss Cochran, was her plane hit?

JACQUELINE: There is no statement of any artillery fire. And you know from your training, Miss Hansen, night flyin' is tracking missions, not firin' missions. The artillery men are only there to track, not fire. Big lights focused on your plane – trackin' your plane - that's all they do.

GERRY: Unless there happens to be a trigger-happy trainee.

CATHERINE: That's enough, Gerry.

GERRY: All I'm sayin' - ma'm - is don't piss on my shoes and tell me it's rainin'.

LIZ: That was uncalled for, Gerry.

GERRY: Miss Cochran comes from my side of the tracks. She knows what I'm talkin' about.

JACQUELINE: You are all dismissed.

GERRY: I want a transfer.

JACQUELINE: Not on your life.

GERRY: You can't stop me.

JACQUELINE: You're right. I can't. But I can delay you.

LIZ: She's not going to resign, Miss Cochran.

GERRY: Since when do you talk for me?

LIZ: We're all a little emotional. We just need some time.

GERRY: Stop talking for me!

JACQUELINE: Miss, Hansen, while I will not give you a transfer, I would be most happy to accept your resignation.

CATHERINE: Resignation?

GERRY: You mean -- I wouldn't fly at all?

JACQUELINE: Not for the military. I think you would be much happier if you did resign. *(Beat.)* You can reach me through the Major. And now if you'll excuse me, Ladies. I have a plane to fly.

CATHERINE: With all due respect, Miss Cochran, Miss Henson has a right to transfer. It's part of the agreement. You informed us at our very first meeting that as civilians we are not obligated to take any assignment to which we do not feel suited. We have that right.

JACQUELINE: Rights exist when you are in the military. You are civilians. You have privileges. And those privileges are at my discretion. I do not suggest you take this path, Miss Henson. It will not serve you. It will not serve our program.

(JACQUELINE exits. A silence follows. CATHERINE moves in the direction of JACQUELINE's exit.)

GERRY: What now?

LIZ: We keep on flying.

GERRY: If some trigger-happy trainee shot her plane down, it should be investigated.

LIZ: You heard Miss Cochran. It was a trackin' mission.

GERRY: Our mechanic suggested otherwise. You said so yourself. *(To CATHERINE.)* Catherine help me out here! *(CATHERINE remains silent.)*

LIZ: No matter what Wayne said, it can't be investigated.

GERRY: We're civilians, Liz.

LIZ: One word gets to the press -- they find out women have been flying semi-combat, this program will blow sky high.

GERRY: So you are agreein' that – maybe - there was artillery fire? Or has the "maybe" changed to "possibly" or "actually" or –

LIZ: *(Cutting GERRY off.)* Nothing has changed. I am simply saying that an investigation would destroy this program. I do not want this program destroyed. We can't let that happen. We've come too far.

GERRY: *You've* come too far! *(Turning to CATHERINE.)* For the last time, Catherine, say something.

CATHERINE: It's complicated.

GERRY: What is so damned complicated?!

CATHERINE: Gerry, you can't always shoot from the hip.

(As GERRY speaks LT. RYDER enters with orders.)

GERRY: I'm not going to keep my mouth shut! I want to know what happened. I want to know why every plane we take up is a deathtrap! I have a right to know.

LIZ: *(Seeing LT. RYDER.)* That's enough, Gerry.

GERRY: *(Not realizing LT. RYDER is present.)* Was her plane shot down?

LIZ: Not now. *(The WOMEN turn to LT. RYDER.)*

LT. RYDER: They've got you ladies scheduled to fly 0700.

GERRY: *(Gently.)* Officer, was her plane shot down?

LT. RYDER: Ask Sugar Charley. I'm G.D.O. Remember?

CATHERINE: *(She realizes that there is a cover up, and she can't stand with JACQUELINE. The anger is not shouted. It is direct.)* You son-of-a-bitch! You never wanted us here! You're glad she's dead, aren't you! Aren't you?!

GERRY: Catherine! Leave him be, for God's sakes! He knows as much as we do!

CATHERINE: Since when are you takin' his side?

GERRY: I'm not takin' his side! I want to know just as much as you do. But he doesn't have the answers! *(To LT. RYDER.)* Do You?

LT. RYDER: *(Looking directly at Gerry.)* It's as if nothin' ever happened, ma'am.

CATHERINE: Lieutenant. What do you mean by that?

GERRY: He doesn't mean anything! Leave him –

CATHERINE: Plenty has happened! And you know more than you are telling. And damn it! We have a right to know!

LT. RYDER: It's hard seeing someone you know die. But you wanted to be here. I hope it was worth it.

CATHERINE: You never wanted to see us fly.

LT. RYDER: True ma'am, but I swear I never wanted to see you dead. *(LT. RYDER starts to exit. LIZ stops him with her question.)*

LIZ: Why do you swear that?

LT. RYDER: It's just an expression, ma'am.

LIZ: No, it is not. The military is very precise.

LT. RYDER: Well, on that matter ma'm, you'll get no argument from me. *(LT. RYDER exits.)*

LIZ: *(After a silence.)* Oh, my God.

GERRY: What's wrong?

LIZ: He swore he didn't want to see us dead.

CATHERINE: Liz, you're tired.

LIZ: These planes are suicide traps. Nobody needs to help them along -- unless they don't like who's flying them. Remember what the Major said -- if we did well, the men would get jealous and want their jobs back?

CATHERINE: You are tired. Now, come on, let's get some rest.

GERRY: Are you saying that somebody wants us dead? Is that what this is all about?

LIZ: I'm saying they want to scare us. Like when they leave bolts on our seats, so they think it's missing a vital part.

CATHERINE: Scare us.

GERRY: Scare us?! They killed one of us. And what about the WAF story -- buzzing someone out of the sky? That's to scare us?

LIZ: I think it was a joke.

CATHERINE: A joke!?

LIZ: A joke that backfired. I think if we blow it out of proportion-

GERRY: Blow it out of proportion?!

CATHERINE: Wait a minute -- slow down -- our close friend just died -- Gerry is not blowin' anything out of proportion.

LIZ: Do you want this program deactivated? Is that what you want. How many casualties have we had in this war? How many? Thousands -- and there's no end in sight. Do you actually think anyone cares about Mary or any other woman or man who dies in what could be classified as a freak accident?

CATHERINE: I don't care what they think. I just want to know if Mary was hit by artillery fire, or if some practical joker sent her to her death. I don't think that is too much to ask.

LIZ: What did Miss Cochran say to you?

CATHERINE: That she's protecting us.

GERRY: And you believe her.

CATHERINE: *(Repeating JACQUELINE'S words but not quite believing them.)* Don't let personal matters get in the way of national concerns.

GERRY: And you believed her? You trust her?

LIZ: If we make any move to find out what happened, we will lose our chance to fly -- lose our chance to help win this war.

CATHERINE: *(Silence.)* You believe that.

LIZ: I do.

CATHERINE: And what if it happens again?

LIZ: We take up another collection, have another memorial service, and go on with this war.

GERRY: You want us to be clay pigeons for some deranged trigger happy artillery trainee?!

LIZ: There's no proof of that!

GERRY: The hell with proof! We're civilians for Christ's sake! There's nobody to protect us!

LIZ: If we're careful, it won't happen again.

GERRY: Mary was careful.

CATHERINE: *(Pause.)* What if it does happen again? What if it were Gerry or me?

LIZ: The program goes on.

CATHERINE: Goes on?

LIZ: Yes.

GERRY: If anything happens to any of us, we just let it go?

LIZ: Affirmative.

CATHERINE: You cannot mean that?

LIZ: I do. We have to fight in such a way that we do not jeopardize the ground we've gained.

CATHERINE: And who the hell do you think you are, Liz? General Patton!

LIZ: And you will make the same promise to me.

GERRY: Look. I didn't get into this war because I wanted to be somebody's experiment. I don't know how you can say that if another incident happens, we're supposed to shut our eyes. It's impossible. I can't imagine stepping into a plane knowing that maybe there's someone out there who wants to scare me, and maybe that joke is going to lead to my death. That's insane.

LIZ: Maybe you should resign.

CATHERINE: What?!

LIZ: This is not a game, or some social event. We're fighting a war.

GERRY: Don't you think I know that? And I want to help, but not if every time I look at a man on this base, I think he's out to get me. Liz, I'm sorry. I don't want to be a hero.

LIZ: I'm not asking you to be a hero.

CATHERINE: What are you asking us to do, Liz? To forget that we're mortal? -- that there's a very thin line between life and death, and we come face to face with that line whenever we take a plane up?

LIZ: I am asking you to do exactly what the men are doing. To fight this war and cover your ass as best you can. Now are you with me or not?

GERRY: No, Liz. I am not with you. You are crazy. You want to gamble with your life? You do that. But leave mine alone!

(GERRY walks over to the downstage left acting area and sits.)

LIZ: Catherine?

CATHERINE: That's not a decision I'm ready to make.

LIZ: Catherine, you will make the right decision. We've come too far for you not to make the right decision.

CATHERINE: Go to hell!

(LIZ looks at CATHERINE who has turned away, then at GERRY. There is a moment. LIZ smiles and exits.)

CATHERINE: That was the last time I saw her. And my last words: "Go to hell." Those three words, the way she looked at me -- a small smile on her face -- that damned smile she always gave you when she felt she had the corner on truth -- the words -- the smile -- they've taken residence in my mind -- and in those quiet hours of reflecting, they surface -- like demons -- like ghosts. *(LIZ enters on the upstage platform walking in slow motion. She stops center.)* I wanted to talk with her the next day. I wanted to tell her that I didn't agree with her, but I wouldn't push for an investigation. But she'd requested a three-day pass, and when she got back, we were on different schedules. I didn't even know she'd gotten married. When I got off duty, I went back to the barracks to find her. Instead, I found you.

(CATHERINE moves into GERRY'S acting area.)

GERRY: I can't... I won't... they can't make me... I'll just pack -- that's what I'll do -- I'll get out of this room -- this base -- I'll get out now. I'll -- oh, I hate it -- I hate it -- it shouldn't have happened -- it should have been –

CATHERINE: Gerry -- Gerry -- are you all right?

GERRY: It's crazy -- there's no sense to it -- I'm not stepping on a plane -- we're civilians, Catherine, we don't have to step on a plane -- right -- right! It's right! We don't! We don't!

CATHERINE: What the hell happened?

GERRY: I hate this barracks, you know. I hate it. You can see planes comin' in on final approach! It's rotten' to be in this room. I've gotta get out. I gotta get –

CATHERINE: Gerry, Gerry -- please -- stop it now! Where's Liz?! I'll go get Liz; we'll all go drinkin' together.

GERRY: No -- no -- you can't get Liz; you can't!

CATHERINE: Gerry -- what are you talking –

GERRY: I saw her. I saw her -- from my window –

CATHERINE: What?

GERRY: It was my assignment. I had to take one of our A-26's. Pick up the new Chaplain and bring him back here. Liz said she wanted to do it. She said she wanted to see how it felt to fly now that she was a married women. So I let her. The CO just called Don.

CATHERINE: *(barely audible)* Oh, my God.

(Pulsating music fades up and under through the scene. GERRY and LIZ speak simultaneously.)

GERRY: *(simultaneous with LIZ'S speech below.)* I was here by the window. She was coming in for the final approach. I saw the plane coming in for landing, and then it went up again.

LIZ: *(simultaneous with GERRY'S speech above.)* Tower – we've got trouble. I'm going to try and land this baby. I need clearance. I'm going to need to make another circle – but something's wrong with --

GERRY: *(simultaneous with LIZ's speech below.)* I thought maybe she hadn't gotten clearance. That's not unusual. Bu then I saw her approach, and I don't know - the plane was approaching too fast – the flaps weren't down – the wheels must have locked! Whells must have locked!

LIZ: *(simultaneous with GERRY's speech above.)* Jesus – what the hell is going on – Christ, fellas, I'm having problems with the – Easy – easy – Tower – Tower – emergency landing – I've got a passenger. *(LIZ continues alone. Calmly smiling.)* Chaplain, sorry about takin' the Lord's name in vain -- gotta a little nervous. My minister always says when you take the Lord's name in vain, you're really cryin' out for help. So -- if you want to send up a more appropriate prayer -- I'm jokin', of course. We'll make it just fine.

GERRY: The plane hit -- nose first! Up in flames -- she didn't have a chance. Not a chance.

CATHERINE: She's dead?! She's -- the accident report!

GERRY: It's not good being here. It's not good. I'm leaving.

CATHERINE: The Form one -- did you see the Form 1!

GERRY: I'm leaving! I'm resigning!

CATHERINE: The Form 1, Gerry! The Form 1!

(WAYNE enters with the Form 1. He is center. JACQUELINE COCHRAN enters stage right.)

GERRY: I'm getting out of here. Out. *(GERRY runs out.)*

CATHERINE: The Form 1! Gerry! *(CATHERINE turns to WAYNE.)* Liz Langley's -- I want to see her Form 1.

(WAYNE hands the form to CATHERINE.)

JACQUELINE: Bring all forms regarding Elizabeth Langley to Major Stephenson's office on the double. This is highly confidential.

WAYNE: *(WAYNE is focused on LIZ as he addresses JACQUELINE COCHRAN.)* Yes, ma'am I'll find the report and get it to you on the double. *(WAYNE takes the form from LIZ.)*

CATHERINE: Sugar in the tank? What the hell is sugar doing in the goddamn tank? It stops an engine dead. She didn't have a chance. They are not going to tell m this isn't sabotage.

WAYNE: *(Overlapping CATHERINE'S last line.)* Here you are, Miss Cochran.

JACQUELINE: *(JACQUELINE takes a moment to read.)* Mister, I want no one to see this. Do you understand?

WAYNE: Yes, ma'am.

JACQUELINE: I do not want my girls getting excited about this incident. I want it kept quiet. The accident report has been filed.

(JACQUELINE tears up the form.)

WAYNE: Yes, ma'am.

CATHERINE: This is sabotage.

JACQUELINE: There has been no sabotage.

CATHERINE: I am not talking about the accident.

JACQUELINE: Resignations will be accepted.

CATHERINE: I wouldn't give you the satisfaction.

JACQUELINE: I cannot have you inciting the other women.

CATHERINE: You can't stop me.

JACQUELINE: Liz would have stopped you. She would not have wanted you to do anything to jeopardize this program. I'm right, aren't I? Perhaps she's stopping you now. Well – *(A long pause as the women look at one another. A light comes up on LIZ. CATHERINE looks at LIZ. LIZ smiles her tight, ironic smile.)* I have a plane to fly. And so do you.

(Music fades under and out.)

CATHERINE: So I flew. For two years, I flew. I flew everything and anything. I'd fly the tow-targets, hoping the trainees would hit the plane. I'd dive bomb - taking chances that I knew were suicidal. I flew in a mindless, fugue state. I talked with no one. Talking was too risky. Talking made it real and making something real is making it true, and there was no truth in this. Because truth is something that must be absolute, and there were no absolutes. There was only a need I couldn't even understand. Keep flying. Keep flying for Liz. And then it was over.

(Lights out on CATHERINE: Lights up on MAJOR STEPHENSON and LT. RYDER.)

MAJOR STEPHENSON: Here are their orders, soldier.

LT. RYDER: *(LT. RYER takes the form and reads.)* It's over, sir?

MAJOR STEPHENSON: Forty-eight hours. You will have the bus take them into town.

LT. RYDER: Permission to speak, sir.

MAJOR STEPHENSON: Granted.

LT. RYDER: They proved themselves, sir. Why can't they just keep flying?

MAJOR STEPENSON: Congress was not aware of this program. That means they hadn't approved the funds, Lieutenant. They don't like surprises. I don't like surprises. And to add insult to injury, Ms. Cochran gave General Arnold an ultimatum.

LT. RYER: Excuse me, sir.

MAJOR STEPHENSON: Yes, an ultimatum. WASPs militarized under her leadership or not at all.

LT. RYDER: Do the women know that?

MAJOR STEPHENSON: In time, I am sure they will. Look, Lieutenant, all this hulabaloo with Congress is a way to end the program. It's been buildin' to that for months now. The men want their jobs back. Besides, the war's goin' be over soon. Time for these ladies to do what they were meant to do – get married, raise families – balance, Lieutenant – balance. That's what our world needs. You'll know that once you're married and see your first born cradled in your wife's arms. You'll see yourself buildin' for their future. It's better this way.

LT. RYDER: Maybe they're showing us they can do both.

MAJOR STEPHENSON: Maybe. But not in the armed forces. No. And, frankly, I don't know how to train women flyers. I don't know what to say to them. When you train men, you tell them you're here to learn to be professional killers, and that could mean dying.

(continued)

MAJOR STEPHENSON (Cont'd): But you're dyin' for a cause greater than yourselves. That's what you say to a man. I couldn't say that to a woman. Now, you issue their orders. You put them on a bus and take them into town. From there, they're on their own.

LT. RYDER: But –

MAJOR STEPHENSON: I repeat. They are on their own.

(Lights down on MAJOR STEPHENSON and LT. RYDER. Lights up on CATHERINE and LIZ dressed as in Act One.)

CATHERINE: And we're still on our own.

GERRY: Sugar in the tank. My God.

CATHERINE: I called Jackie. She called. There were pleasantries, and when I asked her about Liz's death –

(Lights up on JACQUELINE.)

JACQUELINE: That's behind us, Catherine. You want an investigation. That will not happen. And now it is over. Don't you want this to be over? We served our country when they needed us. Dwell on that.

CATHERINE: I asked the men. Everything was classified.

(Lights up on WAYNE.)

WAYNE: Don't know, ma'am. And most likely, we won't ever find out. But if I were a bettin' man, and sometimes I am. Whoever did it -- didn't mean to.

(continued)

WAYNE (Cont'd): It was like those college fellas do -- you know when they get into their fraternities. They do practical jokes, and sometimes people get hurt.

CATHERINE: But the accident report –

WAYNE: Different from Form 1, ma'am -- you'll see that soon. Being typed up now. States this was a landin' accident. Pilot error. What you saw in the Form 1 was -- well -- not part of the accident report ma'am. Censored ma'am. Never happened. With all due respect, ma'am, women shouldn't be doing this stuff, ma'am. Oh, I don't mind if you fly, but not in war, ma'am. It's not good for you. You belong home.

(*Lights down on WAYNE).*

CATHERINE: I talked to a few others. Lt. Ryder…

(*Lights up on LT. RYDER.)*

LT. RYDER: There is nothing to say, Miss Watts. Leave well enough alone.

(*Lights down on LT. RYDER.)*

CATHERINE: Major Stephenson – he wouldn't even talk with me.

(*Lights up on MAJOR STEPHENSON. Lights down on MAJOR STEPHENSON.)*

CATHERINE: Something happened. Sabotage? It doesn't matter. It's not that I don't care. War is about winning no matter what the cost. The cost for me was Mary and Elizabeth... *(Beat)* and you.

(Silence.)

GERRY: I couldn't stay, Catherine. I just couldn't. I'm here now.

CATHERINE: Am I suppose to say "better late than never?

GERRY: I don't want you to say anything.

CATHERINE: Good. I'm all out of words. *(Silence.)* So. What do we do now?

GERRY: Pick up the pieces. Bits and pieces of our lives. Everybody does that after a war. Why should we be different? I ran, Catherine. But so did you. Maybe not right away. But you ran. And you're still running.

CATHERINE: I'm doing just fine. *(CATHERINE opens the palm of her hand. She holds up the wings - a soft laugh and tears.)* We sure went through a hell of a lot for a piece of jewelry.

GERRY: You'll get no argument from me.

CATHERINE: I would from Liz. *(Catherine looks up at the sky.)* Look. The stars are out. See those two stars up. That's Liz. That's Mary. *(Beat.)* I'd like to be alone. You can stay. I just need a walk.

GERRY: Are you sure?

CATHERINE: That I want you to stay? *(GERRY nods.)* Yes. No. In my study there's a scrapbook -- third drawer down. I never forgot. I never forgot what we did. I never will. We were the lucky ones.

(CATHERINE exits. GERRY watches her go. GERRY takes out the wings from her pocket and pins them on her dress. As the she does this, the cast slowly moves into their original positions. The snare drum begins under DONALD'S voice.)

DONALD: On November 23, 1977 -- the day before Thanksgiving, President Jimmy Carter signed Veterans status for the Women's Air Force Service Pilots of World War II. It became a law. They were now considered a part of US military history. On that day, Catherine began her journey - first to Minnesota where she joined Mary O'Conner's parents, brothers, and sisters. They honored Mary's resting place with an American flag. Then Catherine came to my home. Early evening we drove to the cemetery and placed the American Flag on Liz's resting place. The stars were out that evening. It had been 32 years since the War had ended.

END OF PLAY

NOTES

Made in the USA
Charleston, SC
15 August 2016